STEEL

From the Iron Age to the Space Age

STEEL

From the Iron Age to the Space Age

by Douglas Alan Fisher

*Illustrated with photographs,
diagrams, and engravings*

Harper & Row, Publishers
New York, Evanston, and London

CONTENTS

Preface   vii

Part **I**

THE IRON AGE

1. Melting Stones with Fire   3
2. The Iron Age Begins   10
3. Steel in the Ancient World   17
4. The Blast Furnace   20
5. England Takes the Lead   31

Part **II**

THE STEEL AGE

6. Bessemer Process Launches the Steel Age   45
7. Lake Superior Iron Ores   58
8. Andrew Carnegie—Steelmaster   66
9. Alloy Steels, I, Their History   76
10. Alloy Steels, II, Alloying Elements   86
11. Steel in Long Strips Like Paper   96
12. New Processes, New Products   107
13. Automation   122
14. The Revolution of Rising Expectations   128
15. Steel in the Atomic-Space Age   147

Part **III**

A MODERN STEEL MILL

16. From Ore to Iron   159
17. Making Steel   171
18. Shaping Steel   182
Index   197

To Marjorie

PREFACE

Steel: From the Iron Age to the Space Age, as its title indicates, relates the history of iron and steel from ancient times to the present.

The book is divided into three parts—*The Iron Age, The Steel Age,* and *A Modern Steel Mill.* Parts I and II comprise the historical section. Since steel, more than any other industrial metal, has shaped the world in which we live, I have devoted the major portion of the book to its history.

In tracing the development of modern iron- and steelmaking processes, I found no convenient place to describe the sequence of their operations in a steel mill. This I have done in Part III. Here the reader may follow operations in a large, integrated steel plant, from smelting the iron and refining it into steel to the manufacture of steel products ready for shipment to customers.

It is hoped that this book will give the reader a better understanding of the role that steel plays in a modern industrial economy such as that of the United States. The reader will also be able to recognize why many developing nations are eager to start making their own iron and steel so that their people may be healthier, better fed, better clothed, better housed, and may enjoy many other benefits of the mechanized civilization that is slowly but surely spreading around the world.

I wish to thank my friends in the United States Steel Corporation who took time from their busy schedules to make sure that the technology of steel is accurately described in this book. My special thanks go to Phelps H. Adams, Dr. Richard F. Miller, and Harold E. McGannon. I am also indebted to other steel and industrial companies, museums, institutions, and government agencies for helpful information and illustrative material for this book. I am especially grateful to Mrs. Margaret H. Fuller, Librarian of the American Iron and Steel Institute, for aiding me in my research and supplying me with photographs.

DOUGLAS ALAN FISHER

Asheville, North Carolina
August 1, 1967

Part I

THE IRON AGE

1

Melting Stones with Fire

The glitter of a yellow object in the gravel of a mountain stream may have led man to the discovery of his first metal. The discovery took place in the Neolithic period, or New Stone Age. Neolithic man was fond of adorning himself with necklaces, bracelets, and other trinkets made of pierced shells and brightly colored stones. In searching the banks or shallow waters of streams for suitable shells and stones, his eye may have been caught by a shining yellow object. He picked it up and found that it was soft enough to be hammered easily into beads and other shapes. The yellow substance was pure gold and was, generally speaking, the first metal used by man.

He may have discovered it in other ways. Gold is widely distributed in nature and is one of the few metals found in a pure state. Gold is beautiful. It does not tarnish. It is imperish-

3

able. Small wonder that it became man's most prized metal. Only iron in certain times and places, because of its utility, was valued higher—sometimes being worth five times as much as gold.

The Copper Age

In his search for gold, New Stone Age man came across a darkish stone which, after it was hammered, looked like gold. It was copper, which also exists in a free state in nature. The new stone could also be hammered into beads, which were strung with gold and other pretty stones. All metals were "stones" to early man. He had no knowledge of metals, as such.

Still later, primitive man discovered silver, another metal found pure in nature. Silver pins, earrings, and needles have been unearthed in ruins dating from 2000 to 3000 B.C.

After Neolithic man had been using hammered copper for some time, he made the astonishing discovery that when he beat the copper beyond a certain point, it became harder and served much better than stone or flint for spearheads, skin scrapers, and other implements. Hammered copper was the first metal used by man for tools, and marks his advance from a stone culture to a metal culture in almost every ancient civilization. This period is known as the Copper Age. It began at different times in different regions. Its earliest beginnings are traced from 5000 to 6000 B.C., and it ended about 3000 B.C., when the Bronze Age began.

First Smelting of Metal

A number of explanations have been offered for man's discovery of smelting. To smelt, or reduce, an ore means to liberate the metal from its nonmetallic elements by means of heat. One popular story of the first smelting pictures primitive men building a campfire against rocks that were rich in copper ore. The heat melted out some of the copper which hardened after the fire went out. In the morning, the men poking in the ashes found the lump of metal which they recognized as copper. This chance event was repeated a number of times until the men put two and two together and deliberately smelted copper from the ore.

There are several weaknesses to this story, the principal one being the fact that a campfire attains a heat of only 1,100° to 1,300° F, whereas 1,300° to 1,500° F are necessary to melt copper ores in the forms of oxides and carbonates.

The most likely explanation for the discovery of smelting is the use of a pottery kiln, in which the temperature reached nearly 2,000° F. This was higher than was needed to smelt copper from the ore. In fact, copper could not have been smelted without a forced draft, which was the distinguishing feature of the pottery kiln. The necessary air blast was at first blown into the kiln by mouth through clay pipes. Later air was blown in by bellows made of animal skins. Pottery kilns were known to exist at a very early date in the Middle East. Thus it seems fair to assume that the first crude smelting furnaces were adopted from the pottery kiln.

The discovery that certain "stones" could be melted by fire to yield a substance superior to the original stone was one of the most dramatic leaps in the history of mankind. For thousands of years man had labored to shape stubborn stones which were liable to break or splinter in the process. In smelting, the "stone" flowed in a liquid, and after it hardened it could be shaped without breaking. Malleability, that is, the ability to be shaped by hammering, was of great importance in the eyes of the ancients. Moreover, a metal tool was more durable than one of stone. When a stone or flint blade broke, it could not be repaired. But a metal weapon or implement could be re-sharpened or melted down and hammered again.

It is generally recognized that copper was the first metal to be smelted. The origin of metallurgy has been attributed to Sumeria, Egypt, southern Arabia, and Asia. No doubt smelting took place in those regions at an early time. Where it began is not so important as the fact that it began. The present writer is inclined to believe that the homeland of metallurgy was in the Caucasus Mountains between the Black and Caspian seas, a region abounding in minerals, fuel, and water. The art of smelting may have developed there as early as 4000 B.C. By 3500 B.C. the industry was well advanced. From its birthplace, smelt-ing spread down through the Middle East and eastward to India and China. It reached central Europe around 2000 B.C.

The Art of Casting

The art of casting metal followed soon after the discovery of smelting. Casting means to form a liquid substance, such as a metal, into a particular shape by pouring it into a mold where it hardens into the shape of the mold. The first metal to be cast was copper.

The coppersmith and the potter were fellow craftsmen and doubtless often worked together. It would seem likely that the first casting of metal was a cooperative effort of the smith and the potter. Indeed, early metal castings and pottery have been found of identical shape, indicating that the craftsman who prepared the clay for pottery also prepared the clay molds for casting.

Casting represented an important advance in metallurgy. It permitted the shaping of copper and later of other metals into forms difficult or impossible to shape by hammering. Casting was also easier and faster than hammering, especially for products turned out in quantity. The same master mold could be used as a model for making similar molds over and over. Thus casting greatly widened and extended the use of metals.

Copper, both hammered and cast, provided man with a material superior to any he had yet known for clearing forests, building sturdier homes, constructing larger and safer boats, slaying animals for food and skins, and for self-defense. Copper products of the ancient past included knives, axes, arrow points, bowls, pins, rings, and other jewelry, cups, harpoon- and spearheads, and needles quite like those of today.

The Bronze Age

Man's next important stride forward in metallurgy must have seemed like magic to him at first. He discovered that by

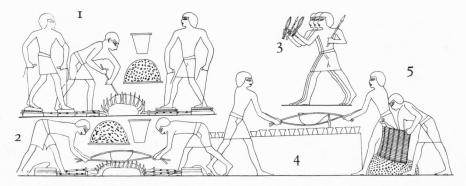

Casting metal. (1) Fire is made to glow by air from bellows worked with the feet and cords held in the hands. (2) Metal is melted in a crucible held over the fire between two rods. (3) Workmen carrying tongs and blowpipes. (4) Molten metal is poured from a crucible into molds, where it cools and hardens. (5) Workman emptying a basket of fuel, probably charcoal. From wall-paintings in the Tomb of Rekhmara at Thebes. Egyptian, Dynasty XVIII (1535–1450 B.C.). *The Metropolitan Museum of Art.*

melting two relatively soft "stones" together, he could produce
a substance harder than either one. He first combined copper
and tin to produce an alloy called bronze. A metallic alloy is a
substance containing two or more metals dissolved or fused
together while in a molten state. Generally there is one principal metal to which a smaller amount of one or more metals is
added. Bronze is roughly 90 per cent copper and 10 per cent
tin. Brass is an alloy of copper and zinc.

Bronze products originated about 3000 B.C. in the Armenian
and Persian highlands, and from there spread out to other
centers. Bronze edges could be hammered thinner and sharper
than copper, and fashioned into knives and forceps, man's first
surgical instruments. Since the art of casting was known,
bronze was cast shortly after it was introduced. Bronze lent
itself particularly well to casting and found its glory in such
objects as statues and works of art. It was also cast into armor,
urns, stoves, keys, ship prows, furniture, ornaments, and other
products.

There was no sharp line between the different "ages" of the
ancient world—the Stone, Copper, Bronze, and Iron ages. Each
came into being in the centers of high civilization in the
Middle East and radiated out to more remote, less civilized
areas. Copper did not at once drive out stone; bronze did not
quickly replace copper; and iron did not banish bronze. One
metal was considered superior to another for certain purposes.
Bronze was tougher and harder than wrought iron and was
preferred for shields through classical Greek and Roman times,
even into the Middle Ages. But the soldier preferred a sword of
Spanish steel if he could get it, because of its sharp cutting
edge. The sequence of ages was not the same everywhere. In
Africa the Iron Age came ahead of the Bronze Age. In other
parts of the world there was no Bronze Age. Some tribes in
Australia and New Guinea still exist in the New Stone Age.

Advances in the Copper and Bronze Ages

The potter's wheel and the smelting furnace gave rise to the first universal crafts. The potter and the smith were highly valued persons, and their services were sought far and wide. Improved tools of copper and bronze brought other craftsmen into being—carpenters, masons, and jewelers. The net effect of better tools was a greater variety and abundance of goods, and larger crop yields, with far-reaching effects on civilization. Transportation and trade were stimulated by invention of the wheel, the basis of mechanization. Population increased; people were better housed in homes of brick, stone, or wood; and communities grew into the first cities.

Hand in hand with economic betterment went advances in cultural and social spheres. Science had its beginnings in mathematics and astronomy, and men reckoned time on sundials. Writing was developed as an economic necessity in order to keep accurate records and accounts in trade and commerce. A livelier exchange of goods required certain standards in weights and measurements.

The advantages of bronze armor and weapons in battle and the growing scarcity of known deposits of copper and tin gave a strong impetus to exploration and trade. Prospectors went west looking chiefly for tin, which was scarcer than copper. Rich veins were discovered in Spain, Bohemia (now in Czechoslovakia), and in Cornwall, England, which served as the principal tin centers for many centuries.

Metals were the main source of wealth and power in the Middle East, and wars were fought over the possession of ore deposits and over metals already mined. The Bronze Age saw the rise of the first great empires—in Sumeria, Assyria, Babylonia, Egypt, Persia, and the realm of the Hittites.

2

The Iron Age Begins

The first iron known to man was obtained from meteorites fallen on the earth. We can only guess when and how the discovery of meteoritic iron may have taken place. A Stone Age man, five to six thousand years ago, searching for stones suitable to make into tools or weapons, may have come across a whole meteorite, or fragments of one, weighing a few pounds. Since a meteorite is largely iron, it would have appeared to the Stone Age man as a dark, almost black, hard stone. He may have managed to chip off a piece or two as a sample. He may have struck the specimen with a stone hammer and discovered that it did not crack or splinter like other "stones," but yielded to the blows of the hammer.

The discovery of meteoritic iron by men in a Stone Age culture may have occurred in other ways. But however it happened, once man learned to beat this tough, malleable substance into sharp points and cutting edges, he valued it above all other materials he had ever known.

Metal From Heaven

Ancient man knew that meteorites fall from the sky. There is unmistakable evidence that he was familiar with "stone showers" from the heavens. In nearly all languages at the centers of high civilization, iron was called "metal, or something hard, from the sky." The early Egyptians named iron *ba-en-pet,* variously interpreted as "marvel from heaven" or "hard stone from the sky." Iron was named *parzillu* by the Assyrians and Babylonians, *barsa* by the Sumerians and Chaldeans, and *barzel* by the Hebrews. A popular translation for these terms is "metal from heaven."

Birthplace of the Iron Age

The total amount of iron that could be obtained from meteorites was small. The metal was extremely rare until man learned that there is an earthly as well as a heavenly iron. The Iron Age is generally regarded as that period when iron was smelted and used on a sufficient scale to affect the course of civilization. There is no question that iron was smelted here and there over a long period, with the secret lost and found again, before the true Iron Age was born. Such isolated smelting of iron undoubtedly took place at an early date in the advanced centers of civilization—Egypt, Chaldea, Babylonia, Assyria, and China. But there is serious doubt that iron was manufactured consistently and on a large enough scale in these areas to constitute the existence of a true Iron Age.

For the birthplace of the true Iron Age, we favor the Caucasus Mountains, which were the home of copper smelting. This position seems reasonable because the smiths there were already highly skilled in the metallurgy of copper. In fact, the first smelting of iron was probably done by coppersmiths who accidentally smelted iron ore for copper ore.

The particular region in the Caucasus Mountains where the Iron Age had its birth was called Chalybia. The Chalybes were famous at a very early time as ironworkers, and were known to have supplied the Greeks with iron.

From its birthplace in Chalybia, the Iron Age is believed to have spread by 1700 B.C. to the Hittites, whose homeland was Anatolia, now western Turkey. By 1600 B.C. the Hittites had obtained a monopoly in the manufacture of iron. If they had learned the trade from the Chalybes, then the Chalybes must have established the first true Iron Age considerably before 1700 B.C. How much earlier? We have no way of knowing.

The Hittites possessed rich and abundant iron ore and became renowned ironworkers. After the destruction of their empire, the Hittite smiths were driven from their homeland. They migrated into the Syrian lowlands, where they were responsible for introducing the Iron Age, about 1400 B.C. The Philistines brought iron into Palestine, where a fairly advanced iron industry existed as far back as 1350 B.C.

By 1000 B.C. the smelting and forging of iron was no longer a secret or a monopoly of any one people, and there was a rush to get into the iron business, primarily for the advantages of iron weapons for warfare.

The knowledge of ironmaking spread throughout the Middle East and to China and India. The Phoenicians and the Greeks carried the art of iron metallurgy westward to Rome and Spain and up into Gaul. The Iron Age was not in full swing in Britain much before 450 B.C.

Early Iron Smelting Methods

In principle, iron smelting is simple. Iron combines readily with oxygen, which explains why most iron ores are oxides and why iron rusts in the atmosphere. Iron ore also contains varying amounts of silicon, sulfur, manganese, phosphorus, and other elements. The smelting, or reduction, of iron ore is based on the attraction of oxygen for carbon under certain conditions of heat. When iron ore is heated in the presence of an abundant supply of carbon-bearing material, such as charcoal, various reactions take place. These depend on the temperature, the proportion of carbon present, and the protection of the iron from direct contact with the air. At the comparatively low temperature of 1,650° F, the iron ore begins to give up some of its oxygen, which combines with carbon in the charcoal to form carbon monoxide gas. When the temperature reaches 2,190° F, a spongy mass of relatively pure iron is formed, mixed with bits of charcoal and waste matter liberated from the ore. This waste matter is known as slag. If the temperature approaches 2,400° F, a radical change takes place. The iron begins to absorb carbon rapidly, somewhat as a blotter absorbs ink, and at this point the iron starts to liquefy. In the smelting process charcoal plays a double role. It generates heat and furnishes carbon for the chemical reaction with oxygen in the ore.

The second, or sponge, stage is as far as the primitive smith got, with some exceptions, in his crude furnace. With a pair of tongs he lifted out the pasty lump weighing about 25 pounds, and hammered it on an anvil to drive out the charcoal cinders and slag and to combine the metallic particles. When the lump became too cool to be worked further, he heated it in a charcoal forge and hammered it again. He repeated this process until the lump was kneaded into a compact mass of relatively pure iron. This was wrought iron, containing from 0.02 to 0.08 per cent carbon. Carbon has a hardening effect on iron. The minute amount of carbon in wrought iron is just enough to make the metal tough and malleable. In the unlikely event that the temperature in this type of furnace approached 2,400° F, the iron sponge would absorb 3 to 4.5 per cent carbon and melt. This is cast iron. So high a proportion of carbon makes iron hard and somewhat brittle. It is liable to crack or shatter under a heavy blow and cannot be forged at any temperature.

The forge was a small furnace in which charcoal was made to burn intensely by hand- or foot-operated bellows. The forge, as its name implies, was used to heat iron to a forging condition, that is, until it was red hot and soft enough to be forged, or shaped, by hammering.

The early iron-smelting furnace was a bowl-shaped hole in the ground, lined with clay. A constant draft was supplied by two or more pairs of bellows made of animal skins, pressed down by the feet or hands. The air was led into the furnace through nozzles, or tuyeres, of clay or bamboo.

Different types of iron-smelting furnaces were developed for local needs. Where there was a steep bank or cliff facing strong prevailing winds, the furnaces were often dug into its side to obtain a natural draft. Sometimes a mound of willow branches was built over the bowl-type furnace and then covered with clay. This type of furnace persisted for many centuries, side by side with more advanced types. It is still common in parts of Africa today.

Gradually the branches and clay were replaced by side walls of stone and the furnace was topped with a stone shaft three to four feet high. Iron ore and charcoal were dumped into the shaft. This process is called "charging the furnace." A fire was lighted and the furnace was kept in operation until a pasty lump of iron intermixed with slag was formed.

New Metallurgical Tricks

Wrought iron was excellent for many purposes, but until the ancient smith learned several new metallurgical tricks, it represented no improvement over copper or bronze because it did not retain a cutting edge. The reason was the small amount of carbon in wrought iron. Moreover, low-carbon wrought iron cannot be hardened by quenching. Quenching means to cool suddenly by immersion in water or oil.

What the ancient smith had to learn was to add enough carbon to wrought iron so that the metal could be made hard by quenching after forging. Quenching was known in very early times. It will harden iron with a moderate amount of carbon. It is possible that in the primitive furnace if the lump of iron was kept sufficiently long in contact with hot charcoal, it might absorb considerable carbon. Then if the smith quenched the iron, he would find that it became hard, and in time he would learn how to produce the same results by trial and error. Or he may have learned the same lesson by repeatedly heating iron in the charcoal forge before hammering it into a tool or implement. The outer surface of the iron would absorb enough carbon from the charcoal for the metal to be hardened by quenching. In other words, the iron had a thin, hard, outer shell, while the interior remained relatively soft. This process is called carburizing.

What frequently passed for steel in ancient times was carburized iron. True steel, however, was made, as we shall learn in the following chapter. At all events, the smith ultimately learned how to smelt iron containing enough carbon for the metal to be hardened by quenching after forging, and also how to carburize it in his forge. He gained insight into another technique. While the quenching of iron makes it hard, it also causes it to become brittle, a highly undesirable property. The iron smelter of early times found out that if he heated the quenched iron to a relatively low temperature, the brittleness was eased without much lessening of the hardness. This process is called tempering.

The Iron Age did not come fully into its own until the

smelter and smith were skilled in five techniques which were unknown to the workers of copper and bronze: (1) adding a correct flux, such as crushed seashells or limestone, to form a slag to take away waste matter in the ore, (2) reheating and rehammering the pasty lump from the furnace to drive out the cinders and slag, (3) carburizing, (4) quenching, and (5) tempering.

Iron's Democratizing Influence

As iron products of the furnace and the forge became more plentiful, their possession was no longer restricted to the rich. It became possible for the farmer to cultivate his land with iron implements and for the carpenter, mason, wheelwright, and other craftsmen to follow their trades with iron tools. Iron became the poor man's friend and had a strong democratizing influence.

"Craftsmen multiply until they cease to be tame purveyors to kings and priests," writes Carleton S. Coon in *The Story of Man,* "and work primarily for the people. Their standards of excellence and their price ceilings are not set by royal overseers, but by their own guild chiefs whom they themselves have elected. Thus during the Iron Age did a middle class grow big enough to produce its own institutions."

The Iron Age not only spread over a wider area than the Bronze Age, but it penetrated much deeper. Iron was welcomed everywhere because it was cheaper than bronze and superior to it for most purposes. It tended to drive out bronze, just as in a much later time iron, in turn, was largely replaced by steel.

3

Steel in the Ancient World

It is not commonly known that steel was made in the ancient world, but numerous records and relics prove that true steel of a high quality was manufactured well before the Christian era. India produced an exceptionally fine steel, called wootz steel. It was shipped to Damascus, in Syria, where artisans fashioned it into the celebrated swords of Damascus. They were so supple that they could be bent from hilt to tip, while at the same time they had a cutting edge that perhaps has never been surpassed.

Manufacture of Wootz Steel

From a description by Aristotle written in 384 B.C. and from later writings, we have a good idea of how wootz steel was made. A special iron ore was crushed into small pieces and sprinkled on a glowing charcoal fire in a small cone-shaped furnace. The draft was supplied by bellows of animal skins, worked by hand. The iron separated from the ore to form a spongy iron lump which was removed from the furnace. The smiths beat the iron lump on their anvils to drive out the cinders and slag. The iron lump was reheated and hammered a number of times until it was as pure as the smiths could make it. Then they beat it into bars 12 inches long and about an inch wide and half an inch thick. The iron bars were cut into smaller pieces and packed in clay crucibles. A crucible is a small pot made of porcelain or other material that can stand a high temperature, and is generally used for melting metals or ores.

Some carbon-bearing material, such as wood, was chopped very fine and mixed with the pieces of iron, and the mixture was covered with two or three green leaves. A clay cover was placed on top of the crucible and carefully sealed with clay to keep out any air. Two dozen such crucibles were shoved into a furnace and heated several hours in a charcoal fire at intensified heat. The iron in the crucibles melted and absorbed enough carbon to become steel. The furnace and the crucibles were allowed to cool down together. As the steel cooled, it solidified. The crucibles were taken from the furnace and broken open, like the shell of a hard-boiled egg, revealing small cakes of solid steel.

The smiths hammered the cakes into steel disks about 5 inches in diameter, weighing from 2 to 5 pounds, and offered them for sale to merchants. This was the original crucible process.

The Persians made steel that was second in renown only to the wootz steel of India. Alternate layers of wrought iron bars and charcoal were heated in a long closed furnace away from contact with the air. The heating continued for ten days or longer, but the temperature was never high enough to melt the iron, as was done in the wootz process. However, the iron absorbed enough carbon from the charcoal to be changed into steel. This was called the cementation process.

In ancient days a third kind of steel was produced, known as "natural" steel. The natural process takes its name from the fact that it produced steel directly from the ore. Only a special kind of ore was used, containing manganese and practically free of impurities such as sulfur, arsenic, and phosphorus. A regular iron-smelting furnace was heated ahead of time for several days. A greater proportion of charcoal and a smaller proportion of iron ore than was ordinarily used in iron smelting were charged into the furnace. A higher temperature also was attained. The greater heat, combined with an excess of carbon from the charcoal caused the iron to absorb sufficient carbon to become steel.

Not only was true steel made in the ancient world, but Greek smiths as far back as the days of Alexander the Great were able to produce different kinds of steel for different purposes. Diamachus, a Greek writer living at the time of Alexander, described three varieties of steel. One was for ordinary tools; a second was for files, augers, chisels, and stone-cutting implements; and a third was for swords, razors, and surgical instruments.

Spain became the leading producer of steel in the Western World, a position she held for many centuries. The chief steel center was Toledo. Some Toledo steel was an alloy steel. Analysis of specimens has revealed the presence of tungsten, manganese, and nickel, all alloying elements used to harden steel. The few Toledo swords that were still being sold in the third quarter of the last century were so elastic that they were sometimes sold in boxes, curled up like the mainspring of a watch.

4

The Blast Furnace

After the collapse of the western Roman Empire in 476 A.D., the iron industry was kept only feebly alive over most of Europe for several hundred years. The exception was Catalonia in northern Spain, where ironmaking continued without interruption. There it was given encouragement by the Moors who dominated large parts of that country from the eighth century until the close of the fifteenth. During the Moorish rule of Catalonia, the Catalan forge was developed. It represented the first important advance in iron smelting since ancient times.

The Catalan Forge

The Catalan forge was usually built against the side of a hill, the hill itself forming the back wall. The hearth was a slightly

20

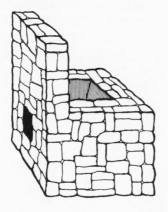

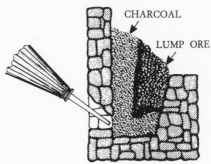

CHARCOAL

LUMP ORE

The Catalan forge represented the first important advance in iron smelt-ing over the furnaces of antiquity. The cross-section diagram shows the method of charging iron ore and charcoal in the hearth, and position of the nozzle, or tuyere, through which the air was driven by bellows. *United States Steel Corporation.*

cup-shaped stone about 30 inches square, built up with stones at the front and on both sides. A short distance above the hearth in the front wall, a hole was made for the entrance of the tuyere to carry the blast from leather bellows.

The hearth was filled with charcoal up to the level of the tuyere. Iron ore was piled in a column at the rear of the furnace, and charcoal was piled in another column in front of it. The smelting process was the same as in earlier furnaces.

The chief advantage of the Catalan forge was its greater productivity. Whereas 50 pounds of iron was formerly the maximum output of a furnace, the Catalan forge could smelt 350 pounds. For this reason it was eagerly welcomed in France and Germany, where is was taken by Spanish ironworkers fleeing the rule of the Moors.

The Catalan forge became the standard furnace throughout Europe during the Middle Ages. Later it spread to all parts of the civilized world where iron was made, even to Japan. In the late nineteenth century the Catalan forge still persisted in its original simplicity in the mountains of Spain and France and also in the United States, where there were two dozen forges of the Catalan type in North Carolina and another dozen in the adjoining counties of Tennessee.

Stückofen and Bloomery

Iron smelters along the Rhine, in an effort to increase the output of the Catalan forge, raised the height of the stone stack, or chimney, to 10 feet and later to 16 feet. This furnace became known as the *stückofen,* because the large mass of metal extracted from it was called a *stück,* which means "piece." In England the taller furnace was called a bloomery, derived from the Anglo-Saxon *bloma,* the term for the lump of iron taken from the furnace.

The *stückofen* yielded an iron mass weighing from 400 to 700 pounds—compared to 350 pounds from the Catalan forge. It required several strong men to lift this iron lump from the furnace, and because it was too large for one smith to hammer, it was cut into two equal parts called *stücke.* Each half was divided into sections small enough for one man to handle and then reheated and hammered into bars for the trade. The annual production of a *stückofen* was from 100 to 150 tons of iron, but it did not work the year round, generally being shut down during dry summer months.

In the earliest *stückofen,* the leather bellows supplying the blast were operated by the hands or feet. Charcoal and iron ore were charged into the top of the stack and more were added from time to time as the smelting proceeded. As the furnace stacks grew taller, they finally were so high that the air blast could not be forced through the deep charge. The problem was solved by the application of water power to the bellows. Water power had been driving simple machines such as grain mills for centuries, but when it was first utilized to operate cams and shafts in more complicated machinery is not known. In the early years of the thirteenth century, water power was driving bellows and hammers in the silver mines of the South Tyrol in Austria, and from there it soon spread to ironmaking regions in Germany and France.

Water-driven bellows were heart-shaped and consisted of wooden boards on the top and bottom. The collapsible sides were made of leather, usually oxhide. The bellows were quite small when first used—about 5 feet long. But as the furnaces grew taller, the bellows grew in proportion in order to provide a blast powerful enough to penetrate the charge. Bellows eventually were as long as 20 feet and as wide as 4 feet at the back. There were usually two bellows to a furnace, each working in turn to supply a steady blast of air.

Water power caused the iron industry to shift its location. Formerly the chief factor in determining the site of an iron-works was the nearness of forests for charcoal. For this reason the furnace was built deep in the woods or on a mountain slope. A certain amount of water was needed for quenching and other purposes, but not enough to turn a water wheel. Now the iron smelters came down into the valleys and built their furnaces on the banks of swiftly running streams and rivers.

True Blast Furnace Is Born

Occasionally the operator of a *stückofen* was surprised to see iron trickle from the bottom of his furnace, where it hardened. Enough heat had been generated in the presence of a plentiful supply of charcoal for the iron to melt. The iron had absorbed sufficient carbon from the charcoal to become brittle and unworkable in the forge at any temperature. Such iron was useless to the smelter who wanted to produce low-carbon wrought iron. The solidified iron mass was, furthermore, a nuisance and a waste of time, since it would have to be returned to the furnace and resmelted. In the early part of the fourteenth century, a new term began to appear among the iron smelters—*flüssofen,* a German word meaning "flow furnace," clearly indicating that it was capable of producing molten iron. It was also known in Germany as a *hochofen* and in France as a *haut fourneau,* both terms meaning "high furnace."

The unwelcome appearance of molten iron running from the furnace presented the iron smelter with a problem until he found a market for his new product. Casting was a well-established industry. Its chief product was bronze church bells. The iron smelter was certainly familiar with the bronze foundry. What could have been more natural than for the iron smelter to begin experimenting with iron castings? It appears most likely that this is what happened and that church bells were the first cast-iron products extensively produced.

Alert to the promising market for cast-iron products, more iron smelters adjusted their furnaces to produce molten iron, and the true blast furnace came into being. It is generally recognized that it was brought to completion in the Rhine provinces, with the Germans, Belgians, and French sharing in this great metallurgical triumph. There is a record of a *flüss-ofen* in operation at Marche-les-Dames, Belgium, in 1340 and of *hauts fourneaux* existing near Liège in 1400. These furnaces were capable of producing molten iron. In 1409 there was a blast furnace in the valley of Massevaux, France, and it is claimed that there were many such furnaces in that country by 1450.

The Tilt Hammer

Water power was responsible for another technological advance in the iron industry—the introduction of a mechanical hammer known as the tilt hammer.

Since the beginning of the Iron Age, the smith wielded a hammer to refine and shape red-hot iron on his anvil. Now the tilt hammer came to his aid, permitting the forging of much larger masses of iron. The tilt hammer was a long wooden arm with a head of iron weighing several hundred pounds. The axle shaft of the water wheel caused the arm to rise and fall, bringing the hammer down with a thundering bang on the hot iron. The tilt hammer could perform the labor of twenty men and greatly increased productivity. It was used to do the first rough kneading of the iron. The smiths still did the finishing work on small sections. In a region of numerous ironworks, there were complaints that the water-driven forge hammers "filled the neighborhood round about day and night with continual noise."

Church Bells and Cannons

The art of casting was developed to a high degree of excellence by medieval foundrymen. They improved casting methods in response to the large demand for church bells during the period of cathedral and church construction throughout the Christian world. Italy and England were especially renowned for their cast-iron bells. Thousands of bells ringing throughout Christendom before the end of the Middle Ages testify to the number and activity of the bell founders. Since they were the most experienced men in casting large iron objects, they were called upon to turn their talents to gunmaking after the introduction of cannons. It was not uncommon for an iron founder to cast bells in peacetime and cannons in times of war.

The first cannons were cast in bronze and are said to have been produced in the city of Ghent in 1313. Soon afterward cannons were made of wrought-iron bars placed lengthwise and welded together with iron rings. Cannons of this type were made larger until eventually they could not withstand the heavier powder charges they required. Besides, their manufacture was too slow and costly to meet the growing demand for ordnance. About 1550 gunmakers switched to cast iron.

The chief concern of the militarist was the cannonball, or shot. The question of a suitable projectile was solved by the adoption of cast-iron balls which could be reproduced cheaply by mass production. Cast-iron shot were produced in such quantity that by the middle of the sixteenth century they consumed more iron than any other product.

The casting of iron cannons became one of the first manufactures in which England excelled. For about two hundred years, the Weald of Sussex enjoyed a virtual monopoly in the casting of iron guns, which were sold all over Europe. The export of cannons reached such a scale in the reign of Elizabeth I that merchant seamen complained to the Privy Council that they were molested and robbed at sea by foreigners armed with English cannons. In response, the ironmasters of Sussex were forbidden to sell cannons abroad except by license, but this and other measures were ignored. Cannons were smuggled out of the country, many of them to pirates hovering in the English Channel. But Spain profited most. When the Spanish Armada sailed forth in 1588 to invade England with the greatest assembly of naval power seen up to that time, most of the Armada's 2,400 artillery pieces were of English manufacture.

Firebacks and Stoves

In the early period of cast iron, its high cost limited it to artillery and to products for the wealthy, but as furnaces grew more productive and economical to run, the price of iron castings fell within the reach of nearly everyone. Cast-iron firebacks became second in importance only to cannons and shot. The fireback was placed at the rear of a large open fireplace to protect the stone- and brickwork from the effects of the fire. In the sixteenth century firebacks were cast by the hundreds of thousands in England and on the Continent. The iron founder took great pride in his designs and indulged his fancy in rosettes, coats of arms, and other ornate figures, many of them of exquisite workmanship. A companion piece of the fireback was the andiron, or firedog, also produced in great numbers. In the seventeenth century firebacks began to give way to cast-iron stoves which became one of the most extensively manufactured iron products in Europe and the American colonies. Other products of the iron founder which opened up large markets were pots, kettles, skillets, gridirons, clock-weights, and cog wheels for machinery.

Direct Furnace Casting—the Cupola

If a large iron casting was to be made, such as a cannon or a ship's anchor, the iron was allowed to flow from the blast furnace directly into the mold. To make smaller castings, such as cannonballs or firebacks, the molten iron was run into a pit, or reservoir. The liquid iron was dipped from the reservoir in a long-handled ladle and poured into the molds. Often the iron in the reservoir would cool and harden before all of it could be taken out. This was wasteful, and it also confined the iron foundry to the site of the blast furnace.

Around 1700 foundrymen in France devised a method to get around these difficulties. The molten iron was allowed to run from the furnace into a sand trough from which it flowed into a number of smaller side troughs. The iron was permitted to harden. The arrangement of the large trough and the little troughs struck the ironworkers as resembling a sow with a litter of suckling pigs. The larger casting became known as a sow and the smaller as pigs and the iron itself as pig iron. The last two terms persist to this day. The pigs were held in reserve until needed, when they were remelted in a separate furnace called a cupola.

The cupola represented an important step forward. The foundry was no longer tied to the site of the blast furnace, though they generally remained side by side for convenience. The cupola allowed pig iron to become an article of commerce. Thus a foundry could exist a short or long distance from a blast furnace, even in a region where no iron was smelted, and have the pigs shipped to it.

Cast iron, because of its high carbon content, is brittle and liable to shatter under repeated hard blows or rough usage. It was an excellent material for products such as pots, firebacks, stoves, and bells, which were not put to usage that might shatter them. But there were numerous iron products such as horseshoes, wagon-wheel rims, plow points, and tools of many varieties whose very function was to stand hard wear and impact. For them cast iron was unsuitable. They required wrought iron.

The problem confronting the ironmaster was to convert brittle pig iron into malleable wrought iron. The excess carbon and various impurities, principally sulfur and phosphorus, were oxidized, or burned, out of pig iron in a charcoal forge called a finery. The finery was filled with charcoal and heated with bellows to a high temperature. Three or four pigs were shoved lengthwise into the glowing fire and stirred with a long iron bar to expose their surfaces to the air blast. The ends of the pigs melted in drops of iron which were changed into low-carbon wrought iron by the oxidizing effect of the air blast.

Forging wrought iron. A white-hot bloom is forged under a tilt hammer into a bar with square ends, called an ancony. The iron head of the tilt hammer is made to rise and fall by the long revolving shaft, turned by a water wheel. The workman wears a broad-brimmed hat, leggings, and apron to protect him from the heat. *Diderot, L'Encyclopedie, 1751, Dover Publications, Inc., 1959.*

The drops joined together to form a spongy lump called a bloom, a later English term for the Anglo-Saxon *bloma*. The word "bloom" became a general term for a large iron mass to be worked into other products.

The bloom was removed from the forge and worked expertly under the tilt hammer into a thick, short, square shape. This was reheated in the finery and again beaten by the tilt hammer, this time until it was a bar about 3 feet long with square knobs at the ends. This was called an ancony. In the final step the ancony was carried to a second forge known as a chafery, where it was reheated and then beaten by hand into bars of different shapes and sizes for sale.

Iron Bar, Standard Product

The iron bar was the standard wrought-iron product sold by the iron industry. It constituted the local blacksmith's stock of iron on which he drew to make whatever products were in demand. He was the local manufacturer from remote times to the Village Blacksmith of Longfellow, and even later, who forged articles for the home, the farm, for other craftsmen, and even for war. In England iron bars were generally sold at the market town or fair. It was customary for the lord's bailiff to buy what iron bars were needed and to have the village blacksmith fashion them into nails, horseshoes, mattocks, hay forks, sickles, bolts, hinges, hoops, and countless other products. "The iron-bound bucket that hung in the well," existed as early as 1331.

5

England Takes the Lead

After the Romans withdrew from Britain about A.D. 410, most of their civilizing influences "fell into oblivion," but one craft remained—that of the smith. The Anglo-Saxons held the smith in such esteem that he was treated as an officer of the highest rank and his person was protected by a double penalty.

Edward III gave strong encouragement to native industries in the fourteenth century by inviting to England craftsmen in various trades from abroad and at the same time restricting imports of foreign goods. He forbade the export of iron from Britain. Under these favorable conditions, the iron industry expanded its activities during Edward's reign, but the metal was still so scarce that the iron pots, spits, and pans in the royal kitchen were classed among the king's jewels.

The low output of iron in medieval England was due to the

continued use of the low bloomery long after the blast furnace
had appeared in France and Germany. It was not until 1496
that a blast furnace was erected in Britain, and then it was
done at the command of Henry VII to cast artillery for an
expected war with Scotland. Other blast furnaces soon followed in the Weald of Sussex, which became the busiest iron
center in Britain. Iron manufacture reached its peak in the
reign of Queen Elizabeth I when instead of importing iron,
England began to export it in large quantities, mostly in the
form of ordnance.

England's Need for Wire

England's chief export and main source of revenue at that
time was wool. Large quantities of iron wire were consumed
annually in "carding" or combing wool to prepare it for
weaving. This was done with "wool cards" containing short
projecting iron wires. England depended almost entirely on
foreign supplies of wire.

For many centuries wire was made by cutting thin sheets of
metal into narrow strips and then hammering them into a
rounded form. The wire industry may be said to date from the
time that man discovered how to form wire by drawing it
through a die. A wire drawing die is a tapered hole of hard
material, larger at the entrance than at the exit. As the rod is
pulled, or drawn, through the die, it is squeezed into the size
and shape of the exit hole and becomes wire.

France was the first nation to develop wire drawing on a
commercial scale, but in the fourteenth century the Germans
took over and made Nuremberg the European home of the
wire industry. Wire was originally drawn through a die by
sheer human force, a few inches at a time. The Germans
invented a machine operated by a hand crank which could

draw wire in lengths of 6 to 12 feet, the ends of which were forged together. Next, water power was applied to the machine, and the modern wire industry was born.

It was her desire to be independent of imported iron wire for the wool trade that led to the erection of England's first water-driven wire mill about 1566, more than two hundred years after it had been introduced in Nuremberg. The British wire industry developed rapidly and became a large and profitable business.

Slitting Mills and Nails

An important step forward in this period was the invention of the slitting mill, the chief purpose of which was to prepare nail rods for the manufacture of the humble but indispensable nail. From remote times to the invention of nail-making machines in the eighteenth century, nails were formed by hand. A narrow strip of wrought iron called a nail rod was cut into sections about the length of a nail. The sections were heated in a forge and then taken one at a time and hammered on an anvil into the shape of a nail.

The nail rods were first laboriously slit by hand from a flat iron bar. Then a great aid came to the nail business. This was a water-driven machine called a slitting mill. A flat iron bar was heated and then cut into strips by passing between a series of revolving disks. Such a mill was known in the Liège district of Belgium around 1500, and the first appeared in London in 1588.

The slitting mill stepped up productivity in nail making tremendously, and for a period nail making consumed more iron than any other product. The booming nail trade had its center in Birmingham where women and girls were employed as "nailers" in numerous blacksmith shops, "wielding the hammer with all the grace of their sex."

Tin Plate and the "Tin Can"

In very early times men knew that tin had a high resistance to oxidation. The Romans coated copper vessels with tin to make containers for food and drink. The modern industry of tin-plating steel can be traced to 1240 when the rich tin mines of the Erz Gebirge Mountains in Bohemia were rediscovered and the tin-plating of iron sheets was developed. The secrets of the process were so well concealed in Bohemia that they did not become known elsewhere in Europe until the seventeenth century.

Plating iron with tin is basically a simple process. The iron sheet is immersed in molten tin, but the trick is to give an even, adhesive coating. The sheet must be smooth and meticulously clean, without a speck of dirt. The iron sheets at that time were hammered by hand, and it was impossible to make them completely smooth. A Welshman, Major John Hanbury, began about 1697 to operate a water-driven rolling mill which produced iron sheets with a much smoother surface than hammered sheets. He discovered that they retained tin-plating very well. Others experimented with tin-plating the sheets and were delighted with their superior quality. Hanbury's rolling mill, the accessibility of tin mines in Cornwall, and abundant water power laid the basis for the rapid rise of Wales as the tin-plate center of the world.

Until this time tin plate had been used in ornamental work and food containers, but never to *preserve* food. Modern canning methods stem from a prize of 12,000 francs offered in 1795 by the French government under Napoleon for a method to preserve food for French sailors at sea. A Parisian confectioner Nicolas Appert, using glass bottles, won the prize. Appert's success aroused the interest of tin-plate manufacturers in Wales, and in 1810 a process was patented for preserving food in cans made of tin plate, and the "tin can" was born.

Wales entered upon a new wave of prosperity as the world's leading supplier of tin plate for the new and growing food-preserving industry, a position it held until overtaken by the United States in the 1890's.

From Charcoal to Coke in the Blast Furnace

From the Bronze Age onward, charcoal had been the principal fuel used in smelting and working metals. The great abundance of forests and the ease of making charcoal favored the use of this fuel. Logs were stacked in a conical pile which was covered with turf except for an opening on top which served as a chimney. There were holes around the base for the admission of air. This mound functioned like an oven. A fire was built inside. Enough air was allowed to enter through the holes in the base to keep the fire smoldering, but not to ignite in flames. The heat of the fire caused the logs to give off their fluids in the form of steam and heavy oils, leaving behind a gray, porous substance that was almost pure carbon—charcoal.

Large quantities of charcoal were consumed by the iron industry—in blast furnaces, fineries, and in hundreds of blacksmith shops where the metal was shaped into needed products. Extensive as were the forests of England, trees were not quickly replaced, and from the fourteenth century onward there were louder and more frequent complaints against the "voracious" iron mills. The shortage of wood for charcoal occurred only in England. There were still enough forests in Germany and Sweden, the chief continental iron producers.

Complaints were loudest against the loss of timber for shipbuilding because "shipping is the walles" which prevented
enemies from invading England. Tough oak was desired for
English ships of war and merchant vessels at a time when the
nation was expanding overseas and clashing with Spain.

When Elizabeth I came to the throne in 1558, she faced a
dilemma. How should she balance the need for timber between
the shipbuilding and iron industries? She enacted various
restrictive measures on the felling of trees, but they were not
rigidly enforced and the English iron industry continued to
devour its own tail. Finally in 1584 the Queen forbade the
construction of new ironworks in the chief ironmaking dis-
tricts.

The tragic result of all these measures was that the iron
industry of England nearly expired. Between 1612 and 1717 the
ironworks of the British Isles shrank from eight hundred to
fifteen furnaces and fourteen forges, or about 96 per cent.
England depended heavily on iron imports from Sweden, with
Russia and the American colonies adding to her supplies.

The man who rescued the English industry from extinction
was a Quaker, Abraham Darby, of Coalbrookdale. A number
of persons before him had attempted to smelt iron with coal,
but with doubtful success. Darby, who knew about the use of
coke in the brewing, dyeing, and brass industries, experimented with using it in place of charcoal in his blast furnace.
We know from his journal that by 1709 he was successfully
smelting large quantities of iron with coke.

Darby is one of the great names in the entire history of the
iron and steel industry. By combining England's iron ore
mines and coal beds, he revived the dying iron industry and
prepared it to rise to new heights of greatness after steam
power ushered in the Industrial Revolution.

The greater productivity of coke-fired blast furnaces led to a
drop in the price of iron, with the result that iron was increas-

ingly substituted for wood, copper, lead, and brass. In less than
one hundred years after Darby's death the world output of
coke-produced iron rose from a few thousand tons to more
than 100,000 tons a year.

The First Rolling Mills

Iron and steel in a red-hot, or forging, condition consist of a
relatively weak mass of crystals. Under the kneading action of
the smith's hammer, the crystals are broken down and elongated into a closely packed bundle of fibers, thereby improving
the quality of the metal. Hand forging had two objectives—to
shape the iron and to improve its quality. Rolling iron or steel
is really a form of mechanical forging.

The remote ancestors of the massive rolls of today's steel
industry were tiny hand-driven cylinders employed by gold-
smiths and jewelers to flatten strips of gold and silver. By the
early seventeenth century the cylinders had grown large
enough to roll lead and tin into flat sheets for making organ
pipes. From then on, rolling mills were improved and grew
larger, and were finally driven by horses or water power.

All these mills were for metals that were ductile enough to
be rolled in a cold condition. It appears that the first rolling of
heated metal was done to prepare flat iron sheets for the slitting
mill. Such a combination rolling and slitting mill may have
existed in England as early as 1588. The rolling mill of Major
Hanbury was an independent machine and not part of a
rolling and slitting mill combination. By 1720 mills for rolling
flat iron sheets were common in England and on the Continent.

Grooved Rolls and Puddling

The next step in the evolution of the rolling mill was
momentous. By constructing rolls with grooves in their sur-

A rolling and slitting mill. The workman flattens the white-hot iron bar gripped in the tongs by passing it through a crude rolling mill. Next the bar is cut into the width of a nail by the sharp disks of the slitting mill at the left. Both mills are driven by a water wheel, shown at the right. *Colonial Craftsmen, by Edwin Tunis, World Publishing Company, 1965.*

faces, it became possible to roll iron into various shapes. The hot, soft metal, in passing between the rolls, was squeezed into the shape of the grooves. In a sense the rolls functioned as mechanical dies.

Many of the world's great inventions were not put into successful commercial form by their inventors but by more practical-minded persons. Such was the case with grooved rolls and the puddling furnace. Henry Cort, an Englishman, invented neither one, but he made them both highly successful.

After some years of experimentation Cort perfected a mill with grooved rolls for producing round, square, and flat iron bars. He took out a patent in 1783. At the same time he investigated an improved method for converting high-carbon pig iron into low-carbon wrought iron. Pig iron as produced in the blast furnace was still being converted into wrought iron in fineries. It was slow work and productivity was low.

Cort experimented with a reverberatory furnace and from it developed the puddling furnace. A reverberatory furnace is one in which the flame is reflected from the roof onto the material treated. In the reverberatory furnace used by Cort, there was no contact between the metal and the fuel, as in the finery. The iron was placed in a separate forward compartment at the base of the flue. Behind the metal, separated by a bridge, was the combustion chamber, filled with charcoal or coal. Flames and gas from the burning fuel, in passing to the flue, swept over and heated the iron, oxidizing out the excess carbon and other undesirable elements, converting it to wrought iron. Heat was intensified by reflection from the roof.

Cort's new furnace, which became known as a puddling furnace, had an opening in the side wall through which a "puddler" stirred the iron with a long rake, exposing all parts of the metal to the oxidizing effects of the flames and gases. When the iron reached a pasty condition, the puddler rolled it into three balls, each weighing about 150 pounds, a convenient size to be lifted from the furnace by tongs. Each ball was put under the forge hammer to expel the slag and form it into two elongated sections, or blooms. While still hot, each bloom was passed through the grooved rolls which shaped it into bars. Cort patented his puddling furnace in 1784.

Although Cort was not the original inventor of grooved rolls or the puddling furnace, he was the first to combine them successfully and for this reason has gone down in history as the father of modern rolling. The effects on the iron trade were impressive. Plants which had formerly forged 10 to 20 tons of iron a week with difficulty, manufactured ten times that amount and with fewer men. Grooved rolls and the puddling furnace brought to an end the long era of the smith's supremacy and inaugurated that of manufacture by machinery.

The Arrival of Steam Power

Thomas Newcomen, a British engineer, is generally acknowledged as the inventor of the first practical steam engine. His engine, patented in 1705, moved a piston connected with a pump and at first was used almost entirely to pump water from British coal mines. In 1764 James Watt was asked to repair a Newcomen engine. He did more than that. He made a new engine with a rotary shaft and gave the world the first steam-driven engine capable of operating various kinds of machinery.

The first use of a Watt engine for a purpose other than pumping water was to blow a blast furnace. This was in 1780. A little later Watt engines were harnessed to drive other blast furnaces and still later to drive forge hammers and rolling and slitting mills. Water power was on its way out of the British iron industry.

The technological advances achieved in Britain—coke blast furnaces, grooved rolls, puddling furnaces, and steam power—produced remarkable results, as may be seen in Table 1.

TABLE I

NUMBER OF ACTIVE FURNACES AND OUTPUT OF PIG IRON
IN GREAT BRITAIN, 1788–1806

Year	Number of Furnaces	Output in Net Tons
1788	85	76,496
1796	121	140,088
1806	173	273,113

Revival of the Crucible Process

The ancient cementation steel-making process was the principal method used in Europe until the "revival" of the crucible process. Cementation steel, because of blisters which formed on its surface, was also known as blister steel. It was not of uniform quality and was often streaked with slag. The best blister steel was made in Germany.

An English clockmaker, Benjamin Huntsman, became dissatisfied with the German blister steel he was importing for his clock and watch springs and sought ways to improve it. He surrounded his experiments with the utmost secrecy. After repeated and disheartening failures he finally produced crucible steel of excellent quality in 1740. He is supposed to have "rediscovered" the "lost" wootz process. It was not lost but was very much alive. Wootz steel was still being imported into England and was so superior to all other steels that die makers were willing to pay the "fabulous" price of 5 guineas a pound for it. A guinea was a gold coin, roughly equivalent in value to the English pound. It is hard to believe that Huntsman did not know of wootz steel, but it may be said that he did "rediscover" the process in that he worked out the secrets himself.

Sheffield, England, was already famous as the world center for fine steel cutlery—all kinds of cutting implements, especially knives. Now the Sheffield cutlers tried to find out Huntsman's secrets. On his guard he forbade any stranger to enter his premises and swore all his workmen to secrecy. As an extra precaution all work was done at night. The story has come down that a spy from the Sheffield cutlers came disguised as a beggar one cold winter evening and asked in pity's name to be allowed to warm himself by the fire. Lying on the floor, he pretended to sleep but slyly watched the operations.

Whether the story is true or not, Huntsman's process was

soon known in Sheffield where more progress was made in steelmaking from his death in 1776 to the close of the century than anywhere else in the world.

The crucible process became the principal method for producing steel until the invention of the Bessemer process in the 1850's. The crucible process made fine steel, but productivity was low and the heavy consumption of charcoal made it costly, all of which explains the need for an inexpensive, mass-production method which the Bessemer process offered.

Liberty and the Industrial Revolution

In the 1,400-odd years covered in the last two chapters, from the fall of Rome to the early nineteenth century, we have passed from a civilization whose roots lay far back in antiquity to the opening phases of the Industrial Revolution. Life in Western Europe moved forward on a broad front. Of all the forces that were active in those often turbulent years, one ran through like a refrain. This was a new concept of liberty held by the common man. It gained its fullest expression in England, as Parliament gained the upper hand in its long struggle with the Crown.

The greater freedom of personal enterprise enjoyed by Englishmen over their fellow Europeans may have had a lot to do with the beginning of the Industrial Revolution in England and the emergence of Darby, Cort, Huntsman, and others, who lifted the iron and steel industry from virtually primitive conditions to a state where it was prepared to take advantage of steam power in the dawning age of the machine.

It was iron, steel, and steam that made Britain the workshop of the world, a position that was not seriously threatened until after 1870 when other nations began to catch up through their own industrial revolutions.

Part **II**

THE STEEL AGE

6

Bessemer Process
Launches the Steel Age

Iron had served man well as his chief industrial metal for
several thousand years, but it more than met its match in the
Industrial Revolution as machinery grew heavier and wheels
turned faster, driven by steam power. Steel was then made
chiefly by the crucible process. Crucible steel was produced
on too small a scale and was too expensive for wide industrial
use. To a degree the Industrial Revolution marked time,
waiting for some modern Vulcan to devise a way to produce
cheap steel by the ton instead of the pound. When Vulcan
appeared, he was a triple personality—William Kelly, an Irish-
American; Henry Bessemer, an Englishman; and Robert
Mushet, a Scotsman.

All three had a hand in giving to the world the Bessemer
process which ushered in the Steel Age. Bessemer's name was

immortalized, and he reaped a fortune equivalent to more than $5,000,000 from the process. Kelly was ridiculed and called a fraud by some of his countrymen, and his name is not connected with the process which he was the first to invent. Neither Bessemer nor Kelly could have made steel with their processes without the contribution of Mushet, who realized only a few English pounds for his part and died a relatively poor man.

William Kelly's "Air Boiling Process"

William Kelly was born in Pittsburgh. In his youth he studied metallurgy to prepare himself for the manufacture of iron. He and his brother John purchased an ironworks near Eddyville, Kentucky, where they produced pig iron in a charcoal blast furnace and converted it into wrought iron in a finery. Their furnace and finery consumed large quantities of charcoal, which they produced from their own nearby woodlot. Within a year or so they had cut down all their timber. The nearest other source was seven miles away, and to haul charcoal that distance would seriously increase their operating costs.

William began to think of ways to save fuel. One day as he sat watching his finery he noticed that the iron directly under the air blast from the bellows was whiter and apparently hotter than the rest. With a shout, he sprang to his feet. He realized that the cold air, instead of chilling the iron, as everyone before him believed, actually made it hotter. His knowledge of metallurgy told him that the oxygen in the air was combining with carbon in the iron to produce heat. He saw the possibility of refining pig iron into wrought iron by means of air alone. In that instant the principle of the Bessemer process was conceived by Kelly. This was in 1847, eight years before the same idea crossed the mind of Henry Bessemer.

Kelly's plan was to force a powerful blast of air on molten pig iron in a specially constructed furnace by what he called his "pneumatic process." When he explained his theory to his friends and neighbors, he was greeted with ridicule and became known as "Kelly, that crazy Irishman." He devoted so much time to his experiments that he neglected the ironworks, and this began to disturb his father-in-law, a Mr. Gracy, who had loaned him money. Finally Mr. Gracy told Kelly that he would have to give up his "air boiling process" or pay his debt.

But Kelly was sure he was on the right track and continued

One of the converters used by William Kelly in experiments with his "pneumatic process." At this stage his converter closely resembled the Bessemer converter as it was finally developed. *William Kelly, by John Newton Boucher, 1924.*

his experiments at a secret location in the woods, where he
built and tore down seven furnaces. When Mr. Gracy learned
of this, he decided that his son-in-law must really be crazy and
he called in a doctor to examine him. After Kelly had explained his theory to Dr. Champion, the doctor decided that
his patient's mind was sound and so was his theory, and he
became one of Kelly's strongest supporters.

Kelly finally succeeded in producing malleable iron by his
pneumatic process in the 1850's and sold his product on a fairly
extensive scale. (Note that he produced iron. He had not yet
produced steel.) He had not patented his invention, wishing to
perfect it further, but when he heard that Henry Bessemer had
obtained an American patent on his own process in November
1856, he applied for one. The question of which inventor had
first claim to an American patent came before the Commis-
sioner of Patents in 1857. Kelly was awarded priority over
Bessemer and was granted a patent. Bessemer's patent was disallowed. One of the witnesses who helped Kelly win his case
was Dr. Champion.

The Role of Henry Bessemer

Henry Bessemer was a mechanical genius and an inventor of
the first rank. His steelmaking process was only one of 110
inventions, some of which were remarkably brilliant. Pure
chance turned his attention to the iron industry in 1854.

Britain and France were then allied with Turkey against
Russia in the Crimean War. It came to Bessemer's attention
that British and French artillery experts wished to be able to
fire a shell a long distance but were unable to do so from a
smooth bore gun. For a shell to travel a long distance with any
accuracy, it must rotate, and this was an effect which the gunmakers at that time were unable to produce. Bessemer applied
his genius to the problem and in short order designed an

"elongated projectile," in his words, that would rotate in a smooth bore gun. But when he reported his device to the British generals, they "pooh-poohed" it, as Bessemer said. Then chance intervened.

Late in 1854 Bessemer was in Paris. He was already a famous inventor. At a house party he attended, he was introduced to Prince Napoleon as the inventor of a new system for firing elongated projectiles from a smooth bore gun. Bessemer happened to have in his pocket a model of his projectile carved in mahogany. He showed it to the Prince, who was fascinated by the toy shell and arranged an audience for Bessemer with his cousin the Emperor (Napoleon III). The Emperor authorized Bessemer to continue his experiments in France, and there in December of that year Bessemer demonstrated that a rotating shell could be fired from a smooth bore gun. "But would it be safe to fire a large shell from a cast-iron gun?" he asked the assembled French officers. "This simple observation," Bessemer wrote later, "was the spark which kindled one of the greatest industrial revolutions that the present century has to record."

Bessemer decided to study the whole question of metals suitable for cannons, which were then made almost entirely of cast iron. He considered that wrought iron or steel would most likely be the best metals for heavy guns. He directed his first researches into iron and within three weeks, on January 10, 1855, applied for a patent.

Bessemer's aim was to make a shortcut in the production of iron and steel. The original charging material for the crucible process had been cementation, or blister steel, but in Bessemer's day it was wrought iron. This was refined from pig iron in a puddling furnace and then rolled into bars. The bars were broken up and heated in clay crucibles, each one holding not more than 40 to 50 pounds. These various steps, from pig iron to the finished crucible steel, took about ten days and consumed immense quantities of fuel. Consequently crucible steel was expensive, selling for the equivalent of several hundred dollars a ton. What Bessemer hoped to do was to jump over these time-consuming and costly steps and convert pig iron directly into wrought iron or steel.

At some stage in his experiments Bessemer developed the same theory as Kelly. Bessemer knew that pig iron contains an excessive amount of carbon—about 4 per cent—as well as certain other elements such as silicon, phosphorus, and sulfur. To convert pig iron to steel, the carbon is reduced through oxidation usually to less than 1 per cent, and the other elements are largely burned out. Bessemer also knew that carbon in molten iron unites readily with oxygen, producing heat. Why not reduce the carbon in pig iron and remove the other un-desirable elements by means of oxygen from a strong blast of air? This was exactly Kelly's idea. But when Bessemer first tried to do this in a furnace he called a converter, he reported that a "veritable volcano" burst forth, with flames, sparks, and smoke beyond his control. After about ten minutes the flames died down, and he poured out the metal and found it to be wholly malleable iron. The converter that Bessemer used was somewhat egg-shaped, with an open mouth and many small holes in the bottom through which the air was blown.

The news of Bessemer's invention burst like a bombshell in British iron and steel circles. The steelmasters of Sheffield at first laughed at the "absurd notion" of producing 5 tons of steel in 10 to 15 minutes rather than 10 days, but they finally came around and asked for licenses to use his process. He charged 10 shillings per ton of metal produced by the process.

Bessemer Is Denounced

All efforts by other steelmakers to utilize Bessemer's process failed disastrously. As failure after failure was reported, the newspapers took up the cry and Bessemer was denounced as a "wild enthusiast" whose invention "like a brilliant meteor, flitted across the metallurgical horizon only to vanish in total darkness." Bessemer realized suddenly the reason for the failures. The other steelmakers had used British pig iron which contained so much phosphorus as to make it unfit for his process. Without being aware of it, Bessemer had used Swedish pig iron which was almost free of phosphorus.

But his faith in his invention was unshaken. He found through chemical analysis that all British pig iron "abounded with this fatal enemy phosphorus, and I could not dislodge it." For more than a year he toiled night and day to get around the obstacle, but without success. One heartbreaking disappointment followed another. He poured large sums of money into his experiments. The steel men jeered at him, and his closest and dearest friends begged him to give up a "pursuit that the whole world proclaimed to be utterly futile."

In the end Bessemer abandoned his efforts to dislodge phosphorus from English iron ore and ordered some phosphorus-free Swedish ore in order to prove to the world the merits of his process. With this ore he produced good malleable iron, but he could not produce steel by his process until he took advantage of a discovery made by the third person in our story—Robert F. Mushet.

Robert Mushet Supplies the Key

Robert Mushet was a partner in a steel company that manufactured crucible steel. He thoroughly understood the metallurgy of iron and steel as it was practiced in his day. On hearing of Bessemer's repeated failures to make steel by his process, Mushet knew at once that Bessemer was trying to solve his problem mechanically, whereas it was a chemical problem. Mushet had learned from his own experience that Bessemer had overexposed his iron to heat and air with the result that the iron contained pockets of oxygen, or, as Mushet expressed it, "occluded oxygen." Furthermore, Bessemer had burned out all the carbon and did not know how to put back the necessary amount to change the iron into steel.

Mushet also knew from experience that "burnt iron," as he called it, could be remedied by adding a compound of charcoal and manganese oxide, then employed in making crucible steel. Later he learned of a better compound called spiegeleisen, containing iron, carbon, and manganese. He tried adding some spiegeleisen to "burnt iron" and converted it into steel. The manganese, having an affinity for oxygen, withdrew it from the iron to form manganese oxide, which passed into the slag. The carbon in the spiegeleisen, meanwhile, remained in the molten iron, adding just enough to convert it into steel. "I saw then," Mushet wrote, "that the Bessemer process was perfected and that with fair play untold wealth would reward Mr. Bessemer and myself." Mushet patented his process in 1856.

Bessemer began to use the Mushet process, but refused to recognize Mushet's patent or pay him any royalties, claiming that a similar process had been known for years. It is generally recognized today that neither Bessemer nor Kelly could have successfully produced steel without application of the Mushet process for adding spiegeleisen.

By 1862 the Bessemer process was firmly established in England, and by 1865 on the Continent, where about 100,000 tons of Bessemer steel were produced in that year.

Bessemer Process Is Launched in America

William Kelly sold the controlling interest in the patent for his process to a group of men who formed the Kelly Pneumatic Process Company in Chicago in 1863, but he retained a small share in the company. The company decided that it would need to use the Mushet spiegeleisen process, and the rights to its use were obtained. An experimental plant was built at Wyandotte, Michigan, and there in 1864 steel was made in the United States for the first time by the Bessemer process.

In 1870 when Kelly applied for a seven-year renewal of his patent, the railroad and steel industries protested against it at the Patent Office, claiming that Kelly was an imposter and that Bessemer was the sole inventor of the process. Since Bessemer's American patent had been disallowed, if Kelly's were not renewed, the railroad and steel interests would not have to pay any royalties for use of the Bessemer process. But all efforts to kill Kelly's patent failed, and in his lifetime he was paid $450,000 in royalties.

From the opposition to Kelly's patent arose the glorification of Bessemer as the only inventor and the downgrading of Kelly as an imposter. The result was that the original inventor's name was all but forgotten. There was another reason, too. At the start most Bessemer steel was imported from Britain and was labeled "Bessemer steel." It became a kind of "brand name" and was easier to sell under that label. Thus Kelly's name gradually faded away and the process became known as Bessemer.

The year 1867 may be taken as the date when Bessemer steel production began on a commercial scale in the United States. A total of 3,000 tons was produced. Within thirteen years production reached 1,000,000 tons, surpassing that of Great Britain for the first time, and in 1899 amounted to 8,500,000 tons.

Bessemer Steel and Railroads

When the Bessemer process was invented, rails were made of wrought iron. The relatively soft rails wore down on one side, somewhat like the heel of a shoe, and had to be "turned" every so often, depending on the heaviness of the trains and the frequency of their passage. Ordinarily rails were turned every six months, but sometimes every three months, and on the sharpest curves as often as every six weeks. The Bessemer process came at a very opportune time, for the railroads urgently needed a stronger metal than wrought iron. But railroad men in England feared that Bessemer steel would be too hard and would not have the give or resilience of wrought iron to absorb the shock of the passing wheels. When Bessemer asked permission of a railway official to install some steel rails on his line, the man replied, "Mr. Bessemer, do you want to see me tried for manslaughter?" The official in the end consented to try one Bessemer steel rail. After two years the steel rail had not been turned once, whereas the adjoining wrought iron rails had been turned seventeen and eighteen times.

This demonstration was enough to convince the most doubting person of the superiority of steel over wrought iron for rails. For many years more Bessemer steel was used for rails than for any other product. It became identified with the railroads in their era of great expansion in England and on the Continent. The improved transportation system had a strong stimulating effect on manufacturing and commerce, and in this way the Bessemer process was an invigorating influence on the trade of the world.

During the period of greatest railroad building in the United States, the fiery Bessemer converters supplied the bulk of the steel for the rails and for the trains themselves. Lines from the East and West were linked together in an historic moment at Promontory Point, Utah, in 1869, completing America's first transcontinental rail system.

The Open Hearth Furnace

The Bessemer process did not have the field to itself for long. In the 1860's a rival appeared—the open hearth furnace. This furnace, as its name implies, converts iron into steel in an "open" hearth, where the steel is exposed to the sweep of the flames. The open hearth process owes its development to the Siemens brothers in England and the Martin brothers in France.

Dr. Charles William Siemens, the elder of the two Siemens brothers, was the first person to advance the principle of the regenerative gas furnace. Such a furnace is based on the fact that hot air will make flames burn with greater heat than cold air. As applied by Siemens, the hot gases from the flames were led through brick chambers which were heated by the passage of the gases. Then cold air for combustion was forced through the hot chambers, taking up some of their heat. This heated air was then united with the flames, causing them to burn more fiercely.

Dr. Siemens patented his furnace in 1861, but he seems to have been unable to make it work successfully. Meanwhile in France, Emile and Pierre Martin were experimenting unsuccessfully with an open hearth furnace. The two pairs of brothers met in France in 1864. Siemens added his regenerative principle to the open hearth furnace of the Martin brothers, and the combination proved to be very successful. It became known as the Siemens-Martin furnace abroad, but in the United States it is more commonly called the open hearth furnace.

An open hearth furnace was installed at the New Jersey Steel & Iron Company of Trenton in 1868, but it was never in regular service. A small 5-ton capacity open hearth furnace, built for the Bay State Works of South Boston two years later, was the first in the United States to operate regularly. Other companies began adopting the new steelmaking process, and by 1880 open hearth steel production amounted to 113,000 tons. By 1900 it stood at 3,800,000 tons, or more than half as much as Bessemer steel.

Bessemer Versus Open Hearth

The Bessemer process had a head start on the open hearth process and maintained its lead in the United States during the last century. But after 1900 the lead began to shorten, and in 1908 open hearth furnaces for the first time poured more steel than Bessemer converters. From then on the open hearth furnace became the leading steel producer, and now accounts for 72 per cent of total steel output in the United States, whereas Bessemer output has dwindled to 0.5 per cent.

The Bessemer process began to lose its once proud position as the premier steel producer because of numerous advantages offered by the open hearth process. The Bessemer converter makes steel in one volcanic rush of about ten minutes. The operation cannot be slowed down or stopped to test the steel and add other ingredients, if needed. When Bessemer steel first appeared, it met practically all needs for steel except those for which crucible steel was still indispensable. Beginning in the present century, the steelmaker called more and more on science to aid him in making steel to meet the stiffer requirements of modern industry. Each batch of steel was made according to precise specifications for its chemical composition. The production of these steels called for furnaces that could be controlled better than the Bessemer converter.

The open hearth furnace takes about ten hours to make a batch, or heat, of steel. This permits removing samples of the molten steel from time to time for testing in the laboratory to make sure the steel is of the correct composition.

The open hearth furnace also answered the need for greater productivity. Whereas the Bessemer converter of 1900 produced 5 to 10 tons of steel at a time, capacities of open hearth furnaces ranged from 15 to 65 tons per heat, with an average capacity of

48 tons. In a word, steel companies turned increasingly from the Bessemer converter to the open hearth furnace because of its versatility, greater capacity, and the generally higher quality of its steel. (The operation of an open hearth furnace is described in Part III, Chapter 17.)

The United States Marches to Industrial Greatness

With Bessemer converters and open hearth furnaces pouring out more steel every year, the United States forged ahead of Britain in 1889 as the world's leading steel producer, a position it has held ever since. Five years later, the United States stood in first place as an industrial power, producing goods double the value of Great Britain's.

The overall growth of the United States in the thirty-three years from the start of the Steel Age in 1867 to 1900 was truly spectacular. Steel production, including all methods, rose from 22,000 tons to 11,400,000 tons, or more than 500 times. Population more than doubled—from 37,000,000 to 76,000,000. The 39,000 miles of railroads spread into a nationwide network of 259,000 miles, stimulating the growth of towns and cities and opening up markets for the products of the farm and factory.

The amount of steel produced per person in a nation is a good key to its industrial activity and living standards. When the Steel Age began, 1.2 pounds of steel were produced per person in the United States. By 1900 the figure had risen to 300 pounds. This meant that year after year more steel was going into factories and their machinery, into trains, ships, buildings, farming implements, typewriters, sewing machines, printing presses, and a host of other products which were improving living standards on a rapidly rising scale.

7

Lake Superior Iron Ores

As the Bessemer and open hearth processes gained headway, pouring out more steel every year, the American steel industry faced up to the problem of obtaining enough iron ore. The industry still depended on local ore deposits, some of which had been mined since Colonial days. But these deposits were relatively small and were totally inadequate for the rising steel demands of the railroads and other industries impatient to grow and expand. The need for iron ore became particularly acute in the dynamic steel center of Pittsburgh.

There was no scarcity of the other two materials for steel-making—coking coal and limestone. Coal was available in the immense seams of the Appalachian ranges, extending from Pennsylvania to Alabama. Limestone, used as a purging agent in the furnaces to carry off waste matter in the form of slag, is a common mineral found abundantly in many states.

58

If the United States was to realize its promise of becoming a great industrial nation, it was essential to have millions of tons of iron ore to draw on. The discovery of large rich deposits in the Lake Superior region was made at a very opportune time.

The Lake Superior region comprises parts of Minnesota, Wisconsin, and Michigan, and also extends into Canada. Iron ore deposits of considerable size exist elsewhere in the United States—in the Northeast, the South, and the West—but altogether they are not as large as the Lake Superior deposits, which have supplied 85 per cent of all the iron ore mined in the United States in the present century. These ores have been the economic vertebrae—the industrial backbone—of America. It is time now to take a closer look at this fabulous iron ore region around the Great Lakes.

Lake Superior Iron Ores

The Lake Superior region includes six iron ore ranges in the United States: the Marquette in Michigan; the Menominee and Gogebic, straddling the Michigan-Wisconsin border; and the Vermilion, Mesabi, and Cuyuna in Minnesota. The Canadian ranges include the Atikokan, west of Lake Superior; the Michipicoten, east of Lake Superior; and the Moose Mountain, north of Lake Huron.

The Sioux Indians knew about "red earth" in the Lake Superior country, and French missionaries who explored its forests and lakes wrote about seeing iron ore there as early as 1660. All this was forgotten for nearly two centuries.

In 1844 the federal government sent a group of surveyors into upper Michigan to mark it out for future townships. Wandering through the forests, the men noticed at one point that their compass needle acted strangely, and suspecting the cause, they found an outcropping of iron ore. This was of little interest to them, so they simply wrote "iron" on that part of the map and went on with their surveying.

On their return to civilization, however, the surveyors apparently talked of their discovery to Indians and later to white men. One of the Indians, a full-blooded Chippewa named Majigijig, investigated the site himself. He stumbled on a mountain of iron ore so large that it filled him with superstitious terror and he fled from the scene. Very likely he associated the iron with evil spirits, as was done by primitive people in many parts of the world. At any rate, Majigijig reported to others what he had seen.

One person who heard the tale was a man named Philo M. Everett, who was then prospecting for gold and copper around Lake Superior. He arranged for Majigijig to lead him to the iron mountain. When they reached a certain point, Majigijig refused to take another step. Pointing westward, he said, "Iron mountain. Indian go no nearer. White man go." This lends further support to the idea that Majigijig associated evil with the iron.

Everett pushed on alone, and in his own words "came to a mountain of solid iron ore, 150 feet high. The ore looks as bright as a bar of iron just broken." He quickly formed the Jackson Mining Company with title to one square mile of land near Negaunee, Michigan. The ore was very rich, but for reasons unknown this first mining venture was not a financial success. In 1849 the Marquette Iron Company was formed, leasing part of Everett's property. This company was successful and shipped the first ore from the Marquette Range—six barrels—in 1852. They were sent to Pennsylvania. This was the first shipment of Lake Superior ore down the Great Lakes.

Other companies became active on the Marquette Range, and ore shipments continued to mount, swollen in succeeding years by shipments from the Menominee, Gogebic, and Vermilion ranges. From six barrels in 1852, iron ore cargoes shipped down the Great Lakes climbed to 7,000,000 tons annually by the close of the century.

The Great Mesabi Range

The Mesabi Range in Minnesota is the largest in the Lake Superior region, and when it was discovered, was the largest known iron ore deposit in the world. More than 2 billion tons of ore have been taken from it. The name Mesabi was derived from the word for giant in the language of the Chippewa Indians.

Various people had explored the hundred-mile long range without profitable results until the Merritt brothers began their famous journeys through the Mesabi territory. Four brothers and three nephews made up the group, but they became known as the Merritt brothers, or The Seven Iron Men. Originally woodsmen, they had made a considerable fortune in buying and selling timber. In 1890 they encountered a body of soft hematite iron ore at a site later to be called Iron Mountain. The ore was so soft that after removing a covering of rocks and soil, it could easily be scooped up by shovels.

When news of the Merritt brothers' rich strike reached the outside world, the Mesabi iron ore rush was on, second only to the California Gold Rush of 1848. Prospectors swarmed over the range, anxious to make a fortune in iron ore. In the early months of 1892, fifty-one companies were formed to mine the Mesabi ores. Before another year was out, shipments amounted to 600,000 tons, and from then on exploitation of the Mesabi belt was in full swing, and in 1902 shipments amounted to over 13,000,000 tons, or more than half of all the ore transported that year down the Great Lakes.

One of the men who heard of the Merritt brothers' discovery on the Mesabi Range was Henry W. Oliver. He lived in Pittsburgh, which Andrew Carnegie had already made famous as the steel center of the United States. Oliver and Carnegie had been childhood friends and messenger boys in the same telegraph office. Oliver's life had alternated between dazzling success, with great riches, and staggering failure. He knew that the booming steel industry needed larger sources of iron ore and that his friend Carnegie, in particular, was unable at that time to get enough for his hungry blast furnaces.

In 1892 Oliver quietly went up to Duluth, the starting-off point for the Mesabi Range. He was not going to join the wild scramble of prospectors. He intended to visit the men who controlled the largest claim—the Merritt brothers. When Oliver arrived in Duluth, the hotels were so crowded with prospectors that he had to sleep on a billiard table. Next morning he bought a horse and rode it through the wilderness to the headquarters of the Merritt brothers. It has been said that from this horseback journey he later realized $13,000,000. When he was shown the loose ore that could be shoveled like sand, he saw at once that he had found what he was looking for. The Merritt brothers were in need of cash to develop their iron ore claims and also to complete a railroad they were building to haul their ore to Duluth for shipment down the Great Lakes. Oliver gave the Merritt brothers a check for $5,000 for certain rights on the Mesabi Range, and in the same year organized the Oliver Iron Mining Company.

On his return to Pittsburgh Oliver proposed to the Carnegie Steel Company that it be given one-half interest in the Oliver properties in exchange for $500,000 to develop the mines. For nearly two years Andrew Carnegie could not make up his mind, but when he heard that John D. Rockefeller was buying up Lake Superior iron ore properties, he made the loan to Oliver, thereby acquiring half interest in the mines.

Rockefeller's big opportunity to buy Mesabi iron ore mines

had come in the panic of 1893 when mining companies were failing or were in desperate financial difficulties. Among those in trouble were the Merritt brothers. Rockefeller bought up vast tracts at very low prices, including all the mines and the railroad of the Merritt brothers, and formed the Lake Superior Consolidated Iron Mines. He now possessed not only a monopoly in oil, but also owned a lion's share of the world's largest iron ore deposit—the Mesabi Range.

Andrew Carnegie did not want to clash with John D. Rockefeller. All he cared about was an assured iron ore supply, so he entered into an arrangement with Rockefeller whereby he leased his properties on the basis of 25 cents a ton of ore shipped down the lakes. Later Carnegie bought five-sixths interest in the Oliver Iron Mining Company. With these two deals Carnegie became master of the Mesabi Range.

Mining and Transportation

When iron ore was first mined in the Lake Superior region, it was dug out of the ground with hand shovels. This became known as the open pit method. Although underground mines were later dug in some parts of the Lake Superior district and elsewhere in the United States, about 60 per cent of all the iron ore mined in the country is still done by the open pit method.

The use of hand shovels was discontinued about 1885 when steam power began to drive large scoops. These were replaced by electrically operated shovels that today can gouge out 20 tons of iron ore in one huge bite and dump it into railway cars. The world's largest open pit mine, the Hull-Rust-Mahoning mine, is on the Mesabi Range. It is probably the largest excavation in the world, about three miles long, one-half mile wide, more than 350 feet deep, and containing more than seventy miles of railroad tracks.

Originally the ore was shoveled into horse-drawn wagons and hauled to Marquette on Lake Superior, where it was transferred by wheelbarrows onto a sailing vessel. When the ship reached the Saint Mary's River between Lake Superior and Lake Huron, the cargo was unloaded and carted in wagons past the rapids in the river and put aboard another vessel. Four to five days were required to unload and reload small vessels at the rapids. This waterway obstacle was finally removed with completion of the Sault Sainte Marie locks, popularly known as the Soo, linking the upper and lower Great Lakes. It was begun as a canal in 1853, but its five large locks were not built until many years later. The Soo handles a greater tonnage annually than any other canal in the world.

A special type of ore vessel was developed to transport ore on the Great Lakes. As the blast furnaces devoured more and more iron ore, larger and swifter vessels appeared on the lakes. A typical ore vessel of today is about 600 feet long and 60 to 65 feet wide, with a capacity of 11,000 to 14,000 gross tons of ore. Some of the giants on the lakes are nearly 650 feet in length, with a breadth of 70 feet and a capacity of 21,000 gross tons of iron ore. Because parts of the water route freeze in winter, the vessels operate about seven and a half months a year. To cut down the "turn around" time of a vessel in port, the loading and unloading methods have been mechanized. In 1905 it took twenty-one hours to load an ore vessel and thirty-three hours to unload. Now the time for each operation is four to five hours.

At the start of mining in the Lake Superior district, it was only natural that the highest grade ores were taken out, ranging from 50 to 60 per cent and more in iron content. These were called direct-shipping ores because they could be used in the blast furnace pretty much as they came from the earth. The higher grade ores have been largely mined out, but billions of tons of low-grade ores exist in the Lake Superior region, enough to last far into the future. The low-grade ores can be treated, or beneficiated, to make them richer in iron content, and are in some respects superior to the direct-shipping ores for the blast furnace. The whole subject of beneficiating iron ores will be discussed in a later chapter, together with worldwide iron ore resources.

With an assured supply of almost limitless iron ores in the Lake Superior region, an abundance of coking coal in other states, and plentiful supplies of limestone, the three essentials in steelmaking, the stage was set for the entrance of the greatest steelmaster of them all, who more than anyone else made Pittsburgh the steel capital of the world, and in the process became the world's richest man—Andrew Carnegie.

8
Andrew Carnegie—Steelmaster

Andrew Carnegie was the greatest steelmaster of all time. More than any single person he brought the United States into the Steel Age.

His first ambition when a small boy was to make enough money so "that saint," his mother, could someday wear a silk dress and ride in a carriage. He realized far more than that. He amassed the largest personal fortune of his time, and after his retirement gave most of it away.

The driving force in this little man—he stood five feet five in his shoes—was a passionate desire to succeed in whatever he undertook. To fail in any enterprise, however small, was for him "an unendurable experience," writes his chief biographer, Burton J. Hendrick. "Merely to achieve first rank was not enough; he must leave his competitors so far behind that they ceased to be rivals."

66

Andrew Carnegie was born on November 25, 1835, in Dumferline, Scotland, the son of a poor weaver. To better their fortunes, the family immigrated to the United States and settled in Pittsburgh. Andy was then thirteen years old.

To help out at home, he went to work in a cotton mill at $2.00 a week. He next became a telegraph messenger boy at $2.50 a week. Always studying for the job ahead, he learned how to operate the keys and was soon hired as a telegraph operator by the Pennsylvania Railroad at a salary of $35 a month. His advance was rapid, and in his twenty-fourth year he was earning the princely salary of $1,500 a year. Already his mother wore a silk dress and rode in a carriage.

Carnegie Enters the Iron Business

Carnegie knew from his experience with the Pennsylvania Railroad that some sections of the line "were fast becoming dangerous for want of new rails." On some of the sharpest curves the wrought-iron rails were replaced every six weeks or two months.

It was Carnegie's awareness of the needs of the railroads that led him in his twenty-ninth year into the iron business. With several partners including his brother Tom, he organized a company to manufacture wrought-iron rails. Within the next few years he formed a company to manufacture locomotives and another company to build iron bridges. To supply his own iron, he and his partners bought two small ironworks and combined them into the Union Iron Mills in 1867. He was now well launched in the iron business.

Carnegie had heard of the Bessemer steelmaking process, which was then used chiefly for making rails, but when a close friend urged him to manufacture Bessemer steel, he brushed him aside with "Experimentin' don't pay."

He was still of the same mind when he went abroad in the summer of 1872 and was given a demonstration of the Bessemer process by the British inventor himself. In the turbulent flames issuing from the roaring mouth of the converter, Carnegie saw a vision of the Steel Age in America. The steamer could not get him back to the United States fast enough. He burst upon his startled partners in Pittsburgh, shouting, "The reign of iron is over. Steel is king!" He urged them to join him in the manufacture of steel, but they refused. They were doing all right in the iron business. Why take a chance on steel? "It required some faith in our star," Carnegie liked to recall in later years.

His First Steel Mills

Faith in his star Carnegie had, and with new partners and $250,000 of his own cash, he formed the Edgar Thomson Steel Company in 1872 and began construction of a plant to make Bessemer steel and roll it into rails. The plant was located at Braddock, near Pittsburgh, where General Braddock suffered defeat and met his death in the French and Indian War.

The Braddock plant was only partially built when the panic of 1873 struck the nation. No longer did the fires from the iron mills around Pittsburgh light the night sky. Gloom was everywhere—in the homes of the business managers and the cottages of the unemployed.

Carnegie bought out his partners in the Edgar Thomson Works, who were only too glad to get out of what they thought was certain failure. Then he scraped together all the money he could lay his hands on and poured it into completion of the plant. In this way he gained control of the company.

When good times returned, Carnegie had the finest Bessemer steel and rail plant in the United States. From the start it was highly profitable. In 1883 there was another depression. Few steel mills were working full time, and many were shut down. Carnegie gobbled up one located at Homestead, near Braddock, at a low price and remodeled it into one of the most advanced steel plants in the world.

The lesson Carnegie learned in installing the latest equipment in the Edgar Thomson and Homestead works became his guiding philosophy, "A perfect mill is the way to wealth." His slowness in recognizing the importance of the Bessemer process was not typical of him. He was eager not only to be abreast of the times, but, as mentioned earlier, to be a step ahead of his competitors.

Carnegie would even scrap a new mill for a better one. When Charles Schwab was president of the Carnegie Steel Company, he once asked Carnegie for permission to build a new mill that would save 50 cents a ton. "Go ahead, Charlie," the steelmaster replied. When the new mill was completed and Carnegie examined it, he saw that Schwab was not satisfied with it. "What's wrong?" Carnegie asked. "If I could build it over again I could save a dollar instead of fifty cents a ton," Schwab answered. "Go ahead. Tear it down," was Carnegie's only comment.

H. C. Frick, the Coke King

The Carnegie Steel Company continued to be very successful, and year after year the profits rose. One man who contributed greatly to its financial success was Henry Clay Frick. Frick had risen from a poor farm boy to the principal owner of the largest coke company in the United States. He was known as the Coke King.

In 1881 Carnegie came to believe that he should control all the raw materials he needed for making steel and decided that he should bring Frick's coke company into his fold. He had long had his eye on the company, but perhaps even more on Frick, who, Carnegie once said, "had a positive genius for management." Carnegie bought a controlling interest in the Frick concern, renamed the H. C. Frick Coke Company. Within a few years Frick was appointed chairman of the Carnegie Steel Company.

Carnegie and Frick needed each other, but their natures clashed and they quarreled frequently. Finally after one bitter quarrel, Carnegie asked for Frick's resignation. Neither man ever spoke another word to the other. At his death Frick left behind one of the finest private art collections ever assembled. It is housed in the Frick Museum in New York City.

Meanwhile, Elsewhere in the Steel Industry . . .

In the last half of the nineteenth century many companies within the same business or industry were combining in what has been termed the consolidation movement. The years 1898 to 1900 saw a stampede in consolidation within the steel industry. The Moore brothers—Judge William H. and James H. Moore—combined 279 tin plate mills into the American Tin Plate Company, and shortly afterward put together three other amalgamations. In the same period the National Tube Company and the American Bridge Company were formed with the financial backing of J. Pierpont Morgan. John W. ("Bet-a-Million") Gates gathered all the wire companies he could buy up and put them together in the American Steel and Wire Company. Judge Elbert H. Gary, a Chicago lawyer, organized the Federal Steel Company with the financial support of J. P. Morgan. It was second in size to the Carnegie company. Judge Gary became its president.

When 1900 rolled around, the American steel industry was

dominated by the following nine large companies. The names of the persons who controlled them are in parentheses.

> Carnegie Steel Company (Carnegie)
> Federal Steel Company (Morgan)
> National Tube Company (Morgan)
> American Bridge Company (Morgan)
> American Steel and Wire Company (Gates)
> National Steel Company (Moore brothers)
> American Tin Plate Company (Moore brothers)
> American Steel Hoop Company (Moore brothers)
> American Sheet Steel Company (Moore brothers)

Competition in the steel industry was severe. It was speeding up the movement toward integration. In integrated operations a company included the mining of its raw materials and the manufacture of its own iron and steel for more efficient and economical production.

The Carnegie company made and sold mostly raw and semifinished steel and such "heavy" products as rails, structural steel, and armor plate. It did not manufacture "light" products such as tubes, tin plate, sheets, and wire, which were the specialties of other companies. In 1900 Carnegie made plans to make tubes by a new process, far in advance of any of its kind in America.

J. P. Morgan Is Disturbed

When the news of Carnegie's tube mill reached J. P. Morgan in his citadel on Wall Street, the great man was highly disturbed, and with good reason. Carnegie's new process would make all but worthless the $80,000,000 which Morgan had invested in the National Tube Company.

But the tube mill was to be only a beginning. Carnegie had bought properties for the construction of mills to manufacture other light products such as tin plate, barbed wire, nails, and still others.

It was widely known that he contemplated retirement, and it has been said that his plan to build a tube mill was merely a device used by the canny Scotsman to bring pressure on Morgan to buy him out. Whether true or not, Carnegie's overall plans constituted a threat to other steel companies, and the battle lines began to take shape for what promised to be a Battle of the Giants.

On one side stood the cocky little Scotsman behind an impregnable empire of steel. He owned three steel mills second to none. He had access to virtually unlimited supplies of Lake Superior iron ore. He owned ore vessels to bring his ore down the Great Lakes, ore docks on Lake Erie, and his own railroad to transport the ores to his Pittsburgh mills. Through the H. C. Frick Coke Company he controlled unmatched deposits of coking coal.

By reason of these physical assets and his own team of young geniuses, as he called his partners, he could produce steel at lower costs than his competitors. He knew his own strength and the weaknesses of his opponents, and they knew that he knew them. In the language of football the Carnegie Steel Company was a precision-drilled team, with an immovable line, masterminded by the smartest quarterback in history, Carnegie himself, and a fleet-footed backfield that could rip holes at will in the opposing team.

On the other side was a group of jittery steelmakers and their lawyers, and in the background loomed the glowering figure of J. Pierpont Morgan, to whom investors were running in droves, begging him to "do something about that mad Scotsman."

One day in 1900 Judge Gary, president of the Federal Steel Company, called on Morgan and suggested that he buy out Carnegie. "I wouldn't think of it," the great financier replied. "I don't believe I could raise the money."

Morgan was of the same opinion when he attended one of the most famous dinners in the history of the American steel industry. It was held in New York, and the guests included the leading figures of American industry and finance. Schwab gave the principal address.

"Schwab," wrote Burton J. Hendrick, "took the assembled bankers to the mountain top and spread before their startled eyes the splendor of his universe of steel. The unfolded prospect was a new and dazzling one." Schwab proposed integrated steel operations on a truly scientific basis, such as had never been done. It would result in such savings that steel could be sold at lower prices. But what he had in mind, he warned his listeners, was not a monopoly, restricting output and raising prices, which he condemned as little less than an industrial crime.

Morgan was deeply impressed by what he heard and afterward drew Schwab aside and talked to him earnestly. Events moved swiftly. At an historic meeting in the library of the Morgan mansion in New York, Schwab was asked again to explain himself. He now set forth his encyclopedic knowledge of the steel business. Morgan never missed a word. As dawn was breaking at the library windows the banker said, "Well, if Andy wants to sell, I'll buy. Go and find his price."

Schwab took the news to Carnegie. After a short discussion Carnegie took a pencil and sheet of paper and jotted down the figure of $400,000,000, saying, "That's what I'll sell for."

When the paper was shown to Morgan, he said, "I accept." In this simple manner was one of the world's greatest business transactions concluded.

Morgan entrusted to Judge Gary the task of rounding up the companies that would accomplish the kind of integration which Schwab had proposed. They included the nine companies previously listed. Morgan was the financier and Judge Gary the organizer of what became the United States Steel Corporation. Gary was appointed its chief executive officer and Schwab its president.

U. S. Steel was incorporated on February 25, 1901, with a capital stock of $850,000,000, raised shortly afterward to $1,100,000,000. It was the largest steel manufacturer in the world and the first billion-dollar corporation in American history.

It's Disgraceful To Die Rich

Andrew Carnegie once remarked to a friend that he should consider it disgraceful to die a rich man. After his retirement Carnegie's main concern was how he could best help mankind with his great wealth.

Recalling how he had thirsted for knowledge as a boy and his difficulty in getting books, he began building libraries. By 1919 he had built 2,811, of which 1,946 were in the United States and the rest in Canada, Great Britain, and other English-speaking countries.

To encourage the pursuit of science for the improvement of mankind, Carnegie founded the Carnegie Institution in Washington. He also created the Foundation for the Advancement of Teaching, whose main purpose was to provide pensions for teachers in institutions of higher learning. He gave money to build the Palace of Peace and the International Law Library at The Hague, in the Netherlands, and established the Carnegie Endowment for International Peace. He remembered Dumferline, his birthplace, "the most sacred spot on earth to me," by giving it $4,000,000 "to bring into the lives of the toiling masses of Dumferline more sweetness and light."

Besides erecting a library in Pittsburgh, he gave the city an art museum and concert hall. He built Carnegie Hall for concerts in New York City.

He established a pension fund for retired employees of his own company, and this fund is still being administered by the U. S. Steel Corporation.

He endowed the Carnegie Hero Fund to reward persons for acts of unusual bravery. He also gave benefactions to hundreds of individuals.

Finally, he gave his remaining fortune, except 10 per cent for his family, to establish the Carnegie Corporation of New York. It spends the income from the endowment, giving money mostly to colleges, libraries, and institutions of scientific and educational research.

The towheaded weaver's son who landed on the cobblestone streets of New York in 1848 could not have foreseen in his wildest fancy how his adopted land would change in his lifetime, nor how he, more than any single person, would move it ahead into the Steel Age.

Shortly before his death on August 11, 1919, Carnegie asked his secretary, "How much money did you say I had given away, Poynton?"

Proud of his memory for figures, Poynton replied, "$324,-657,399."

"Good Heavens!" Carnegie chuckled, "where did I ever get all that money?"

9

Alloy Steels, I
Their History

The Bessemer process, followed shortly by the open hearth process, introduced the Steel Age in the last century by making it possible to produce inexpensive steel in mass quantities. This was carbon steel, a term which means steel as it is refined from pig iron, without any special additions.

Carbon steel is made in three principal grades. Low carbon steel contains under 0.2 per cent carbon, medium carbon steel from 0.2 to 0.6 per cent carbon, and high carbon steel from 0.6 to 1.8 per cent carbon. By varying the amount of carbon and by heat treatment and other processing methods, carbon steel can be given a wide range of properties, from fairly soft to extremely hard.

Carbon steel, in its various grades, was well adapted to most purposes for which steel was used. But toward the end of the last century and particularly in the early part of the present century, demands were put on carbon steel that it could not meet. In numerous applications carbon steel, like iron before it, failed where severe stresses were encountered. A metal of longer-wearing qualities for gears, crankshafts, ball bearings, and other machinery parts was needed. There was also need for a metal that could perform at high temperatures and resist corrosion in steam turbines, oil refineries, chemical plants, and other fields of industry. That metal was alloy steel. Alloy steel was not new, but it was not manufactured on a large scale and in many varieties until the first quarter of the present century.

An alloy steel is a carbon steel to which one or more alloying elements have been added, thereby improving existing qualities and imparting new ones and thus virtually creating a new metal. Although alloy steels constitute only a relatively small percentage of total steel production in major steel centers throughout the world, a modern industrial economy could not carry on without them. In the United States alloy steels average about 10 per cent of total steel production, and in Canada about 5 per cent. In view of their importance, alloy steels deserve a closer look. First, let us briefly review their history.

Faraday, Pioneer of Alloy Steels

We begin, oddly enough, with one of the first forms of steel known, the famous wootz steel of ancient India. This steel was still being made even one hundred years ago and shipped to England, where some manufacturers found it superior to all other steels for sharp cutting edges. One manufacturer of surgical instruments and cutlery, advertised that his products were made of wootz steel, which he "preferred to the best steel of Europe."

The unusual properties of wootz steel excited the curiosity of several men with scientific inclinations. One of them showed a specimen of wootz steel to the great English scientist Michael Faraday. He is best known for his discovery of electromagnetic induction, which laid the basis for the modern electrical industry. He was also a noted chemist.

Faraday analyzed the wootz steel specimen and found that it contained aluminum and silicon. He concluded that it was an alloy steel, and, his scientific curiosity aroused, he applied the full power of his genius to a study of alloy steels. The results of his researches entitle Michael Faraday to be called the Pioneer of Alloy Steels.

His systematic investigation of twenty different alloying elements laid the groundwork for the development of modern alloy steels, including corrosion- and heat-resistant steels, high-speed tool steels, and others, some alloyed with no less than nine elements. He left behind seventy-nine specimens of alloy steels.

Robert Mushet and Machine Tools

Until the invention of steam power, machinery was made of wood except for some iron joints and fittings. But wood lacked strength and was too cumbersome and heavy for fast-moving machinery. Iron replaced wood in machines. To cut out and shape wooden machine parts was not too difficult, but it was another matter when it came to shaping machine parts made of iron. Each part was made and shaped by hand. Production was slow, but worst of all, each handmade part varied slightly in measurement from others of the same kind. For iron machinery to function properly, the parts had to be made to precise measurement. To produce accurate machine parts, the cutting tools themselves had to be driven by machinery, called machine tools.

The potter's wheel is the remote ancestor of the machine

tool. Clay is mounted on the surface of a rotating wheel, and the potter shapes the clay by the pressure of his hands. The ancients applied the same principle to shaping wood by holding a chisel against a revolving wooden bar. Such a revolving implement is called a lathe. With improvements the lathe has continued in use ever since.

When iron replaced wood in machinery, attempts were made to do part of the shaping on a lathe, the chisel being held in the hand. But the human hand could hold a metal-cutting tool against a spinning piece of iron for only a few minutes at a time. Yet thousands of parts were needed for steam engines and the mechanisms they propelled. For the Industrial Revolution to maintain itself and advance, one of the most urgent needs was for the invention of steam-driven machine tools on which the cutting implement was mounted.

The man who rose to the occasion was an Englishman, Henry Maudslay, who before his death in 1831 invented all the basic forms of machine tools—lathes, drills, planers, punch presses, gear cutters, and others. What he did was to substitute a "mechanical contrivance in place of the human hand for holding, applying, and directing the motions of a cutting tool." Automatic machine tools, developed in America to produce interchangeable parts, laid the basis for mass production.

The cutting parts of machine-driven tools had to be made of a particularly hard steel that would not lose its cutting edge too quickly. High-carbon steel was tried at first, but it proved to be unsatisfactory. Robert Mushet, who came to Henry Bessemer's rescue with spiegeleisen, was the first person to develop alloy steels for machine tool parts on a commercial scale. He stands second to Faraday in the early history of alloy steel.

Mushet's alloy steel, containing 7 per cent tungsten, made it possible for the cutting tools to turn 50 per cent faster than with carbon steel. Within a few years his tungsten alloy steel was being used in almost all the engineering workshops of the world, and was the forerunner of modern high-speed tool steels. Progress in tool steels was rapid, and by 1890 tool steels with 18 per cent tungsten and 4 per cent chromium had been developed—the same proportion as in most high-speed tool steels today.

Manganese and Silicon Steels

The third-ranking name in the history of alloy steels is that of Robert Hadfield, an Englishman. As a youth of twenty-two employed in his father's steelworks, he conducted experiments for the purpose of producing a very hard steel for trolley-car wheels. He discovered that, whereas steel alloyed with 3 to 7 per cent manganese was too brittle to be of any use, if he raised the manganese content to 10 or 15 per cent, an entirely new kind of steel could be produced.

Manganese alloy steel combines a number of mechanical properties possessed by no other material. It does not have a particularly hard surface when first made but has the peculiar property of acquiring hardness under repeated impact. For this reason Hadfield manganese steel has won a special place for itself. Did you ever wonder how a power shovel can stand repeatedly knocking against stones and rocks as it gouges out tons of earth? The jaws, lips, and teeth of the shovel are made of manganese steel. The same metal takes similar punishment in bulldozers, dipper dredges, ore crushers, and other earth-moving equipment.

Another contribution of Hadfield was the invention of silicon steel, which became of great importance to the electric industry. This steel had 1.5 to 5 per cent silicon and was very hard. He sold it widely to toolmakers, for at first he had no idea of silicon steel's magnetic properties.

In the 1880's the young electric industry operated at low efficiency, and the cost of electricity was high. This was due mostly to the unsatisfactory material used in the cores of the transformers and generators, which caused a large loss of energy. After it was discovered that Hadfield's silicon steel greatly reduced energy losses, it was adopted for the cores of transformers and generators.

The importance of silicon steel sheets to wider consumption of electricity throughout the world can hardly be exaggerated. Since they came into general use, research has improved the performance of electrical sheets at least 70 per cent, resulting in drastically reduced costs of electricity to industrial users and consumers.

Chromium and Nickel Steels

After it was proved that chromium alloy steel made superior armor plate for battleships, a fresh race in armaments was touched off, mostly between France, England, and Germany, with the United States watching on the sidelines. The race was really carried out in metallurgical laboratories. As one nation developed a thicker, tougher armor plate, others had to come up with an improved armor-piercing shell that could penetrate it. Then a still tougher armor plate had to be found. And so it went on, with particular rivalry between 1877 and 1886, opening up a new phase in naval tactics and teaching metallurgists many things they had never known before. The metallurgists discovered the usefulness of nickel for toughening steel, and they found that a combination of nickel and chromium in steel was even better.

These advances in alloy steels were made for purposes of war, but they paid off later in peacetime applications. Germany forged a nickel steel crankshaft for the steamship *Deutschland* in 1899, and in 1893 the same alloy steel was applied to parts of the electric generator at Niagara Falls. Power shovels with manganese steel teeth dug most of the Panama Canal from 1904 to 1914. The Wright brothers' plane, the *Kitty Hawk,* which made the world's first powered flight, contained nickel-chromium steel in some of its parts, as did the *Spirit of St. Louis,* which Charles Lindbergh flew from New York to Paris in 1927.

At the start alloy steels were produced in small quantities. Each batch was usually for a single product—that is, until after a young automobile manufacturer named Henry Ford attended the Vanderbilt Cup Race in 1905. One of the racing cars smashed up in front of him. He picked up one of the parts and was curious to know why it had not been damaged. He had it analyzed and found that it was a vanadium alloy steel.

Ford wanted to have the steel duplicated and asked several steel companies to take a try at it, but they could not be bothered experimenting in alloy steels. Finally he found a steel company that would listen to him, and after a year's experimentation it produced the first chrome-vanadium steel poured in the United States. Ford placed an order for $8,750,000 worth of the new steel and by this act personally raised the alloy steel business from small lots to a tonnage basis. With alloy steel he not only made longer-wearing gears and other engine parts, but he also reduced the weight of his car by one-half because of the stronger steel. All the other automobile companies were quick to follow Ford's lead.

Stainless Steel, the Glamour Metal

For many years men had sought a metal as rustless as gold but with the strength of iron and steel. In the absence of such a metal they protected iron and steel with coatings of paint, zinc, tin, and enamel. All these coatings have serious drawbacks. Their protection is superficial and of little value if the material is subjected to any wear or rubbing, or if a cutting edge is desired. For steel to resist corrosion satisfactorily, the protection must be within the steel itself. The metal that surpasses all others in this respect is stainless steel.

The "stainlessness" of stainless steel is due to the presence of chromium. Oxygen in the atmosphere forms a transparent microscopic film on the surface of stainless steel. This film acts as a protective barrier against the attack of corrosive agents. Nickel is also present in some grades of stainless steel, but they all contain chromium.

The discovery of stainless steel was not made by any one person, although that claim has sometimes been advanced. Its discovery was the work of a dozen men in France, England, Germany, and the United States. It took place during the first quarter of the present century.

Commercially, stainless steel was born and reared in the cutlery trade of Sheffield, England. It is still prized in knives, carving sets, and tableware. Next to automobile trim, the largest use of stainless steel strip is for cutlery and household products such as coffeemakers, electric grills, toasters, sinks, dishwashers, and other appliances.

Stainless steel first gained recognition in the United States in the chemical industry. Its use spread to other industries where severe corrosive conditions exist—petroleum refining, pulp and paper making, textiles, dyes, rayon, and many others. Stainless steel drums and tank cars are used for the shipment of acids, foods, and products of the beverage industry.

Stainless steel has great strength in addition to being corrosion resistant. These two properties make it an ideal material for streamlined trains—beautiful in appearance, longer lasting and light in weight, and hence capable of greater speeds. The trucking industry utilizes these two advantages of stainless steel—greater payloads and longer life service.

The smooth surface of stainless steel contains no tiny pits, invisible to the eye, where contaminating matter may reside, and it therefore can be easily cleaned and sterilized. This characteristic of stainless steel makes it the most widely used metal for hygienic and sanitary purposes. In hospital operating rooms, gleaming stainless steel is everywhere—the operating table, basins, cabinets, implements. Elsewhere in the hospital it is in every ward—in refrigerators for storing serums and blood, oxygen therapy equipment, incubators for premature infants, and furniture. It is of special importance in maternity and contagious wards.

For similar reasons stainless steel has no equal in food-handling and processing equipment. In many food-processing plants from the time the raw materials enter until they are canned or packaged, they encounter only stainless steel equipment. Food processing must be done by a metal that allows the food to retain its original flavor. Such a metal is stainless steel. It protects the purity and flavor of milk in milking machines, piping systems, pasteurizers, and packaging machines. Many states require that milk be processed in stainless steel equipment. Stainless steel also serves as a sanitary guard in restaurant kitchens, ship galleys, lunchroom and drugstore counters.

Another valuable property of stainless steel is its ability to stand both very high and low temperatures. For this reason it finds wide application in sterilizers, aircraft exhaust systems and combustion chambers, and in tanks for storing liquefied gases at temperatures as low as $-425°$ F.

Stainless steel's beautiful appearance and its nontarnishing property which permits economy in maintenance have won a place for the metal in the architecture of buildings, both inside and out.

High-Strength Low-Alloy Steels

Numerous other alloy steels have appeared. One noteworthy series is called high-strength low-alloy steels. Their original purpose was to save weight in transporation. The stronger a steel is, the less of it needs to be used, say in a passenger train or truck, permitting a greater payload to be carried with the same motive power. Some alloying elements are expensive and add considerably to the cost of steel. It would be a simple matter to use certain high-alloy steels for weight-saving purposes in a streamlined train or a bridge, but such steels would be too expensive for widespread use in heavy equipment.

By combining several less expensive alloying elements in small proportions, metallurgists developed steels that still have great strength. They became known as high-strength low-alloy steels. These steels have permitted the reduction in weight of freight cars by 10,000 pounds and a saving of 30 per cent in the weight of railway passenger coaches, without sacrificing safety or strength. High-strength low-alloy steels are advantageously used in gasoline and garbage trucks and in earth-moving equipment, such as bulldozers, road graders, ditchers, and others. They also fulfill their purpose in buildings and bridges.

10

Alloy Steels, II
Alloying Elements

When we passed from the Iron Age into the Steel Age, we moved into a largely carbon steel civilization. But for the past half century we have been moving even faster into an alloy steel civilization, and the pace will quicken in the years ahead. Alloy steels will assume greater importance in the manufacture of space vehicles, military missiles and rockets, supersonic aircraft, high-speed trains, turbine-driven automobiles, and the construction of atomic reactors, as atomic energy is increasingly used as a source of power.

All these applications can be expected to put extraordinary demands on alloy steels and cause their production to increase at a faster rate than that of carbon steels. The result will be a correspondingly greater increase in the consumption of alloying elements.

The United States must import a metal that is second only to iron in the manufacture of steel, and that is manganese. An average of 13 pounds of manganese is used in the manufacture of every ton of steel to remove excess oxygen and sulfur. Large quantities of manganese are also consumed as an alloying element.

Other important alloying elements are chromium, cobalt, molybdenum, nickel, silicon, tungsten, and vanadium. Boron, niobium (columbium), copper, and titanium are of secondary importance. Of the eight most important alloying elements, the United States is fully self-sufficient in only three—molybdenum, silicon, and vanadium. Silicon is abundant everywhere in rocks and sand and presents no problem. Due to an extensive government program in recent years, the United States now produces about half of its tungsten needs and 10 per cent of its nickel requirements. Supplementary supplies of nickel can be had from neighboring Canada, but the other imported alloying elements must be shipped by sea over long distances. Sea traffic flows freely in peacetime, but if it were ever cut off for a considerable period, the United States and Canada would be seriously handicapped.

The reserves of alloying elements, with the possible exception of tungsten and niobium, are considered adequate for the peacetime needs of the Free World. But in case of war some of these metals would be in short supply.

Alloying Elements
Characteristics, Applications, and Sources

Boron

Symbol	Atomic Number	Atomic Weight	Melting Point (°F)
B	5	10.811	4,192

Boron intensifies the degree that a steel may be hardened, that is, the depth to which it can be hardened by heat treatment. Boron is effective in very small doses—as little as 5/10,000 of 1 per cent (0.0005%) in steel can produce the same results as more expensive or scarcer elements. It thus makes possible the conservation of nickel, chromium, or molybdenum.

Boron is obtained from borax. The world's largest deposits of borax are in California.

Some typical products of boron steels are machinery parts, power-shovel buckets, and diesel-engine crankshafts.

Chromium

Symbol	Atomic Number	Atomic Weight	Melting Point (°F)
Cr	24	51.996	3,430

Chromium is one of the most important alloying elements. It surpasses all others in making steel resistant to corrosion and is present in all stainless steels. It also fortifies the strength of steel at high temperatures and is added to all heat-resisting steels. Small amounts of chromium improve the hardening and wearing properties imparted to steel by heat treatment. Large amounts impart corrosion and heat resistance.

Chromium is an important element in high-speed tool steels, in armor plate and other military equipment, and in a long list of steels for machinery parts.

The United States relies on the Republic of South Africa and on Rhodesia for a little more than half of its chromium ore imports. Imports from the Republic of South Africa have declined slightly in recent years while rising in like proportion from the U.S.S.R., which is now in third place as a supplier, furnishing nearly one-quarter of American imports. Other sources are the Philippines and Turkey.

Ewer, or jug, made of copper and covered with antimony to imitate silver. Egyptian, Late Old Kingdom. (2500-2200 B.C.) *The Metropolitan Museum of Art, Gift of Edward S. Harkness, 1926.*

Bronze statuette of Athena flying her owl, probably found at Athens. Greek, fifth century B.C. *The Metropolitan Museum of Art, Dick Fund, 1950.*

Cape York meteorite, named Ahnighito by the Eskimos. The largest meteorite in any museum, it weighs 34 tons. From meteorites man obtained his first iron, which he called metal from heaven. *The American Museum of Natural History.*

Primitive iron-smelting furnace. The type of furnace pictured here has existed since ancient times and is still used in parts of Africa and India. With long sticks the men work the bellows in and out, supplying the air blast. The furnace yields 5 to 6 pounds of iron per charge.

Blacksmith sign representing St. Eloy, patron saint of hammersmiths. He is standing on an anvil. The sign is made of wrought iron and is 10 5/8 inches tall. From Alsace, seventeenth century. *D. and J. de Menil.*

Fireback, made of cast iron. Firebacks were placed at the rear of large open fireplaces to protect the stone and brick work. French, sixteenth century. *The Metropolitan Museum of Art, Dodge Fund, 1906.*

Wrought iron gate. From Middle Ages onward, European smiths produced beautiful works of hammered wrought iron. Great skill was required to shape the iron quickly while it was still hot. This gate is from eighteenth century France. *The Metropolitan Museum of Art, Gift of Henry G. Marquand, 1888.*

Two early Bessemer converters in blow, as drawn by an artist in 1886. The Bessemer process ushered in the Steel Age. *Reprinted from Harper's Weekly, April, 1886, by special permission.*

William Kelly. *United States Steel Corporation.*

Henry Bessemer. *United States Steel Corporation.*

Andrew Carnegie. *United States Steel Corporation.*

Open pit iron ore mine in the Great Lakes District. Large shovels scoop up the ore and dump it into mine cars, drawn up the steep slopes by locomotives. *United States Steel Corporation.*

The *Thomas W. Lamont* leaves Duluth with 14,000 gross tons of iron ore for a trip down the Great Lakes to an unloading port. *United States Steel Corporation.*

Horseless carriages. Early automobile bodies were made by hand in carriage shops. Frames were wooden, later wrapped around by steel sheets. Two smaller models are seen at the rear. *General Motors.*

Automation requires higher education for steelworkers to keep up with advanced technologies. Free educational classes, including college courses, are given by many steel companies. Here student steelworkers take their final exams. *Automobile Manufacturers Association.*

An ore vessel is unloaded at the raw materials storage yards by four electric unloaders, which dump iron ore near the dock. There two electric ore-bridges transfer the ore in clam-shaped buckets to storage bins. Behind the bins are two blast furnaces, each with four round-topped heating stoves. Light-colored bins at right are nearly empty of limestone. *United States Steel Corporation.*

Coke ovens. Pushed from the oven, coke falls in a fiery cascade into a hot car, which takes it to a quenching station. Coal is charged from a bottom-dump car through a hole in the top of each oven. Between each pair of vertical metal strips at right is a coke oven. Ovens are narrow for quick penetration of heat. *United States Steel Corporation.*

Twin blast furnaces. Each furnace has three round-topped heating stoves to heat air for the furnace blast. Skip cars climb the inclined skip hoist and dump raw materials in the furnace top. Large pipes at the top carry off an immense volume of gases. *United States Steel Corporation.*

Casting a blast furnace. Molten iron pours from a blast furnace in a glaring white torrent. At the end of the trough the iron flows into an insulated bottle car, which keeps the iron molten during delivery to steelmaking furnaces. The workman wears special clothing to protect him from the heat and sparks of iron. *United States Steel Corporation.*

Open hearth furnace receiving a charge of molten pig iron for refinement into steel. The huge ladle is slowly tilted by an overhead electric crane to pour out the metal. A workman signals to the crane operator in his booth, not visible in picture. *United States Steel Corporation.*

Tapping an open hearth furnace. Steel at 3,000° F gushes from the furnace into a ladle. The slag spills over the side at right. *United States Steel Corporation.*

Electric furnace. The furnace can be tilted forward to pour molten steel into a ladle. *United States Steel Corporation.*

Teeming. Molten steel is poured, or teemed, from a ladle into ingot molds. The workman holding the rod opens and closes a hole in the bottom of the ladle, filling each mold with steel. In the mold the steel hardens into an ingot, the first solid form in which most steel is made. *United States Steel Corporation.*

Stripping ingots. After the steel has solidified in the ingot molds, the molds are lifted, or stripped, from the ingots. Massive pincers grip lugs on each side of the mold for this purpose. The row of hot ingots is a glowing cherry-red. *United States Steel Corporation.*

Blooming mill. The white-hot ingot is passed back and forth between the rolls a number of times. After each pass the rolls are brought closer together, finally reducing the ingot into a bloom, 9 inches square in cross section. *Youngstown Sheet and Tube Company.*

One of the engineering marvels of the steel industry—a continuous hot-strip mill. In the six powerful finishing stands the steel moves at speeds up to 3,500 feet a minute. The man in the covered platform stands behind an instrument panel by which he controls operation of the mill. *United States Steel Corporation.*

Structural steel. Steel is rolled in structural forms with cross sections shaped like the letters H, I, U, Z, and other irregular designs. The extraheavy H beam, shown here, is being cut to proper length after leaving the rolling mill. *United States Steel Corporation.*

Space-Age yardstick. Two of nineteen stainless steel forgings for a machine to measure rocket weights and the force of rocket thrusts. Each forging weighs 50,000 pounds, and was shaped in a 10,000-ton hydraulic forging press. *United States Steel Corporation.*

Wire drawing. The steel rod is squeezed through the front end of the die and comes out as wire. The revolving reel, or drum, pulls and winds the wire. *United States Steel Corporation.*

Cobalt

Symbol	Atomic Number	Atomic Weight	Melting Point ($°F$)
Co	27	58.9332	2,723

Cobalt is a comparatively rare element in the earth's crust, estimated to make up only 0.001 per cent. Its important ores are seldom found in sufficient quantities to be mined for cobalt alone. Consequently cobalt is obtained chiefly as a by-product or co-product of other metals, mostly copper.

The main use of cobalt is in magnet steels and permanent magnet alloys. In World War II cobalt first gained recognition as an alloying element in steel for high-temperature service, and since then its consumption has increased greatly. Cobalt steel also serves well in high-speed machine tools that must hold a cutting edge at high temperatures. Cobalt also gives a hard surface to steel for parts of equipment that must resist hard wear.

The largest known commercial reserves of cobalt are in the Republic of the Congo, which formerly produced fully 85 per cent of the world's supply as a by-product of copper mining. This explains the struggle which has gone on in that country in recent years over its mineral wealth. In spite of the political and economic unrest in that nation, accompanied by the destruction of mining equipment, it produced 60 per cent of the world's output of cobalt in 1964. Canada is a large producer of cobalt, where it is a by-product of nickel-copper mining in the Sudbury district of Ontario.

The United States continues to import most of its cobalt from the Republic of the Congo, with lesser amounts from West Germany and Norway.

Niobium (Columbium)

Symbol	Atomic Number	Atomic Weight	Melting Point (°F)
Nb (Cb)	41	92.906	4,380

Niobium has become a valuable ingredient in superalloys for severe high-temperature service, particularly in jet engines, boilers, tubing, and gas turbines. It is also added to certain grades of stainless steel when it is to be used at high temperature or welded.

Brazil is the chief supplier of niobium to the United States, with Nigeria in close second place.

Copper

Symbol	Atomic Number	Atomic Weight	Melting Point (°F)
Cu	29	63.54	1,981.4

Copper is used in small amounts—usually under 0.5 per cent—to retard rusting in steel. The chief use of copper-bearing steel is in products exposed to the weather, as in corrugated sheets for roofing, siding, and drain pipes. The steel industry also uses copper as a protective coating for steel wire and other products. From the standpoint of quantity consumed, copper is one of the least important alloying elements.

The United States is the world's largest producer of copper. Other large producers, in the order named, are U.S.S.R., Chile, and the Republic of the Congo.

Manganese

Symbol	Atomic Number	Atomic Weight	Melting Point (°F)
Mn	25	54.9380	2,273

An average of 13 pounds of manganese is used in making a ton of steel. It will be recalled that Henry Bessemer was unable to remove excessive oxygen and his "dreaded enemy" sulfur from his steel until Robert Mushet came to his aid with spiegeleisen. Spiegeleisen is a metallic substance containing manganese, which has a powerful attraction for both oxygen and sulfur, combining with them and carrying them away in the slag. Today ferromanganese is generally used to "purge" steel of oxygen and sulfur. Only a minute amount of the manganese remains in the steel. For its role in steelmaking, there is no satisfactory substitute for manganese.

If more manganese is added to the steel than is needed for a purging action, some of the metal remains as an alloying element. In quantities of 1 to 2 per cent, manganese increases the strength and toughness of steel. If the proportion is raised to 12 to 14 per cent, as Robert Hadfield discovered, an "entirely new kind of steel" is produced. High-manganese steel is unexcelled for conditions of hard-wearing and abrasive action with repeated impact, as in railway frogs and switches and earth-moving equipment.

Because of its double function in steelmaking, manganese is a very important element to the steel industry. Yet no major steel-producing nation in the Free World possesses large deposits of high-grade manganese. The United States has enormous deposits of low-grade manganese ore, averaging from 5 to 15 per cent manganese. Imported ore averages 45 per cent manganese. To mine American ore and treat it to raise its manganese content to 45 per cent would make it cost two and even four times as much as imported ore.

More than half of the world reserves of high-grade manganese ore lie within the Soviet Union, which produces close to half of world output. Other large producers are in the order named: the Republic of South Africa, India, Brazil, China, Gabon, Ghana, Ivory Coast, and the Republic of the Congo.

Brazil is the chief supplier of manganese ore to the United States, furnishing 25 per cent of its imports, but more than half of American imports comes from the African nations named above. The remainder comes chiefly from India.

Molybdenum

Symbol	Atomic Number	Atomic Weight	Melting Point (°F)
Mo	42	95.94	4,760

Molybdenum is among the top three or four alloying elements. The United States is self-sufficient in this element, producing 70 per cent of world output from mines in Colorado.

In small percentages molybdenum improves the hardening qualities and shock resistance of some steels which find wide use in automobile parts. If higher percentages are added, the steel gains in hardening properties and in combination with other elements is used in high-speed tool steels. One of the greatest values of molybdenum is the strength it imparts to steel for high-temperature service, and for this reason molybdenum-bearing steels are used in steam pipelines, boilers, tubing for aircraft fuselage, and turbine blades for jet engines. Molybdenum is present in certain stainless steels and in superalloys designed for severe high-temperature service. The element also finds use in steel for ball bearings.

Nickel

Symbol	Atomic Number	Atomic Weight	Melting Point (°F)
Ni	28	58.71	2,651

Ever since the naval armament race of the 1880's, which showed the world the extraordinary degree of toughness and strength that nickel could add to steel, no element has been found to excel it for these properties, while at the same time making the steel ductile. This combination of characteristics ideally suited nickel steels for the industrial needs of a mechanized society. Steels containing small amounts of nickel and also, as a rule, some chromium and/or molybdenum have given dependable service in mechanisms of many kinds subjected to repeated stress. Nickel lengthens the life and increases the dependability of gears, crankshafts, ball bearings, and other vital parts of machines for transportation on land, at sea, and in the air, and also for farm and factory machinery and oil-drilling tools.

High percentages of nickel add to the corrosion resistance of chromium steel and fortify its strength at high temperatures. By virtue of these properties, nickel is present in many grades of stainless steel and in heat- and acid-resisting steels.

At the other end of the temperature range, in subzero climates and in artificially created low temperatures, down to $-300°$ F in liquid air machinery, nickel steels are able to perform when ordinary steels are apt to become brittle and crack.

The United States has been pushing its own nickel production program for some years and now fills around 10 per cent of its needs from mines in Oregon. For most of this century Canada has mined the bulk of the world's nickel and furnishes about 90 per cent of American imports. Most of the remainder comes from Norway.

Silicon

Symbol	Atomic Number	Atomic Weight	Melting Point (°F)
Si	14	28.086	2,605

Silicon improves the magnetic characteristics of steel and is used chiefly in steels for electric equipment. Silicon steel is manufactured mostly in the form of sheets, called electric sheets, and as such has figured prominently in the growth of the electric industry as the main supplier of power in modern industrial society.

After oxygen, silicon is the most abundant element in the earth. It is found widely in sand and rocks.

Titanium

Symbol	Atomic Number	Atomic Weight	Melting Point (°F)
Ti	22	47.90	3,300

Titanium was regarded as a metallurgical curiosity until World War II. After its unusual properties were fully appreciated, it underwent a spectacular development, prompted chiefly by the U.S. Air Force. Titanium is 40 per cent lighter than steel and 60 per cent heavier than aluminum, yet its alloys approach the tensile strength of most alloy steels. The main use of titanium is in high-speed aircraft, missiles, and space vehicles.

Titanium is relatively unimportant in the steel industry. It is added to some stainless and heat-resisting steels when they are used at high temperatures or welded. It is also used to increase the strength of some superalloys for severe high-temperature service.

The United States is the world's leading producer of this element. It is extracted and processed chiefly in New York, Florida, and Virginia.

Tungsten

Symbol	Atomic Number	Atomic Weight	Melting Point (°F)
W	74	183.85	6,170

Tungsten has the highest melting point of any metal and is extremely hard. When alloyed with steel, tungsten is unsurpassed for adding hardness which is retained at high temperatures. These properties have made tungsten almost synonymous with tool steel, although most modern tool steels also contain chromium. Some are also alloyed with molybdenum and vanadium.

The largest and richest tungsten reserves in the world are in mainland China. The second largest are in the United States, followed by South Korea.

The United States supplies about half of its tungsten needs from California and Colorado. Imports come chiefly from Bolivia, South Korea, Peru, and Portugal.

Vanadium

Symbol	Atomic Number	Atomic Weight	Melting Point (°F)
V	23	50.942	3,150

Vanadium is one of the major alloying elements in which the United States is self-sufficient. The United States is also the world's largest producer and consumer of the metal.

Vanadium steel was brought into the automotive industry by Henry Ford and it is still used in automobiles. It is also now used in low-alloy structural steels and high-speed tool steels. The chief effect of vanadium is to improve the heat-treating characteristics of steel. It may be used alone, but it is generally combined with chromium, nickel, boron, and tungsten.

Colorado is the leading vanadium ore producer in the United States, followed by Utah and Arizona.

11

Steel in Long Strips Like Paper

In the second half of the last century new marvels and wonders kept coming every year or so from the brains and hands of inventors. You could hear a person talking to you over a wire from miles away, and you could sit at home and read the newspaper after dark by artificial light in a glass bulb just as well as in daylight. There were talking machines and typewriters and many other inventions that took your breath away.

The electric trolley that went faster and was more dependable than horse-drawn omnibuses was the last word in transportation. And then someone invented the horseless carriage that tore along at 15 to 20 miles an hour, endangering life and limb and panicking horses.

The early automobiles were quite literally "horseless carriages" with a gasoline engine mounted in a horse buggy. The first job of the car makers was to build a motor that did not break down on nearly every journey and could be relied on to propel the vehicle and passengers up a moderately steep hill. Since the body was literally a horse buggy, it was natural that it was built by carriage makers. The wooden bodies were given several coats of varnish. Counting the time consumed between coats, it took ten to fifteen days for the painting operation alone.

The carriage makers could conceive of the automobile only in terms of a horse carriage, and they persisted in designing bodies that were suitable to be drawn by horses but not to be propelled by an engine which drove them faster than a horse would ordinarily trot. The early motors produced a great deal of heat which warped the wood and weakened the glue. The roads being mostly unpaved and full of ruts, it is small wonder that the body joints gave way, dreadful creaking developed, and the panels sometimes split.

The body makers at first tried to remedy the situation by fastening sheet steel over the wooden dashboard and hood, then over the doors, and later wrapping it around the rear of the car. Steel was added little by little until the wooden frame was completely covered with sheet steel.

The All-Steel Automobile

The man who may properly be called the Father of the All-Steel Automobile was one of America's great industrial pioneers, Edward G. Budd, of Philadelphia. His interest in the automobile grew out of his work in shaping steel sheets in stamping presses. This was done by pressing a die with strong force on a steel sheet. The resulting product was called pressed steel.

At that time steel was shaped by three principal methods—rolling, casting, and forging. Very little shaping was done by means of stamping presses. But there was an increasing demand for steel products lighter in weight than forgings or castings. This demand was met by pressed steel sheets, which were manufactured into clocks and many articles of the hardware trade, whose chief center was in New England.

Budd, when a young man, was employed in a sheet-metal stamping firm in Philadelphia. While working on an order for pressed steel sheets to cover wooden automobile bodies, he conceived the idea of the all-steel car. His employers saw no future in such a car and believed it was safer to stick to wooden bodies, but Budd had a "vision" and to pursue it, he left his job and in 1912 organized the Edward G. Budd Manufacturing Company, with thirteen employees. Now known as The Budd Company, it employs nearly 15,000 people and is a large manufacturer of automobile bodies and parts, stainless steel railway coaches, and a wide variety of other products, with branches in Canada, Europe, and South America.

Budd's ideas were revolutionary. He saw steel not as a covering of a wooden frame but as a structural material to provide both skin and framework. The flexibility of steel would permit it to absorb the jolts of travel, and greater strength could be realized with less weight. But Budd's proposed all-steel bodies were not welcomed by most car makers, and the young company had tough going for a time. Finally Budd found sympathetic listeners in the Dodge brothers, John and Horace, who were metalworkers themselves and original thinkers like Budd. They gave him his first large order for cars with all-steel body frames. This was the open "touring" type with a collapsible tarpaulin top. The Budd all-steel car eliminated the long, tedious painting job, which was a serious obstacle to volume production. Since there was no wood in the body, it was possible to bake enamel on the steel frames, which gave a black finish of pleasing appearance and of greater durability than varnish. More efficient production at lower cost put the Dodge car ahead of all competitors.

In 1919 directly after World War I, Budd introduced the all-steel, all-welded sedan, while other companies were still making what was called the composite car of wood covered with steel sheets. The majority of automobile manufacturers still viewed the all-steel car with suspicion, if not outright hostility. The car business was booming. Production of passenger vehicles rose from 1,650,000 in 1919 to over 3,600,000 in 1923. The equipment of car manufacturers was designed to make the composite car, and some of the car makers had invested heavily in hardwood forests to ensure a sufficient supply of timber. To change over to all-steel construction would mean installing costly new equipment and for some companies a heavy loss in timber investments. Some ex-carriage makers denounced the all-steel car as "ridiculous" and "cheap" and maintained that thin sheet steel construction would not be strong enough.

In spite of its many advantages, the all-steel car was adopted slowly by the automotive industry and did not become standard until the middle 1930's. In 1910 eleven different steels were adequate for building a motor car. Year by year new varieties were introduced, including alloy steels. Today about 75 per cent of a passenger car is steel, requiring over 160 different types of steel. The automotive industry is the single largest consumer of steel and takes on the average about 20 per cent of total American steel production.

"Give Us Sheets of Uniform Quality"

The ex-carriage makers are not to be blamed entirely for the slowness in adoption of the all-steel car. The steel industry at that time was not equipped to produce sheets on a volume basis of the quality desired by the automotive world. The car makers complained about the uneven surface of the sheets and their lack of uniformity in gauge (measurements) and ductility. Paint or enamel does not adhere well to an uneven surface. Proper ductility was needed for stamping the sheets into body parts.

These defects of sheets were due to the method of manufacture. They were rolled on hand mills, which had undergone little fundamental change since Major Hanbury introduced them to the Welsh tin-plate trade in the late seventeenth century. Because the sheets were hand-rolled, each lot varied from another in dimension and ductility. More than one thousand hand mills were struggling to supply an industry where standardization of parts was of the first importance.

"Give us sheets in long lengths of uniform quality!" was the cry from the automobile makers.

The answer was the continuous hot-strip mill, one of the engineering marvels of the steel industry. The terms "sheet" and "strip" may be confusing. They are both thin, flat steel, and their differences are largely in dimension, which need not concern us here. For our purpose we may look upon them as the same product. First, let's take a look at the hand sheet mills.

Hand Sheet Mills in Operation

A hand sheet mill originally consisted of a single pair of rolls or two sets of rolls, the first doing the preliminary rolling and the second the finishing work. A man called a roller was in charge of the entire operation, assisted by nine helpers.

The following is a description of a mill with two pairs of rolls, known as a two-stand mill. The operation began with a "sheet bar," so named because it was a bar that was to be thinned down into sheets. It was about 30 inches long, 8 inches wide, and ¼ inch thick, and was very heavy. The sheet bar was heated in a furnace until it was red hot. It was carried on long-handled tongs to the first set of rolls, called the roughing stand because the first rough work was done there. A workman, known as a rougher, lifted the bar in his tongs and inserted it between the revolving rolls. As it came out on the other side it was grasped in tongs by another workman, called the catcher. He lifted the bar over the top of the rolls and let it slide back to the rougher. The rougher, meanwhile, had not been idle. He had started a second bar through the rolls, and then as soon as that was done he seized the first bar being returned to him and put it through the rolls for a second "pass."

In this way the two bars were kept going through the rolls, back over the top and through the rolls again. The men worked together in perfectly timed rhythm. It was heavy work, performed in such intense heat that it gave the men a year-round "sunburn."

The bar became more and more like a sheet. A third man stood on a stand near the top of the rolls and with sheer human force turned a great wheel that operated a mechanism which brought the rolls a little bit closer together. Thus at each pass through the rolls, the bar was squeezed thinner and at the same time elongated—in a word, it became more like a sheet.

By the time the bar had become a roughly formed sheet, the metal had cooled too much for further rolling. The sheets were reheated in the furnace and then carried to the second, or finishing, stand. Here, the rolling process was repeated until the sheets were reduced to the thinness desired. A crew of ten men could produce 1 ton of sheets per hour.

It is understandable why sheets from hand mills had an irregular surface finish and varied in dimension. In no other rolling operation did the human factor enter so much. The space between the rolls was adjusted according to the roller's judgment. There could not possibly be the same accuracy in hand rolling as could be achieved by mechanized control. That is why no two lots of hand-rolled sheets were identical and why automobile makers complained about them.

All sheets were made of iron until 1876, when Andrew Carnegie produced the first steel sheet bars at his Edgar Thomson Works.

The Continuous Hot-Strip Mill

As far back as 1865 efforts had been made to roll steel in a continuous process by having it pass through one pair of rolls after another, each set of rolls reducing it a little in thickness, instead of passing the steel back and forth by hand through one pair of rolls. Considerable progress had been made, and by the early years of this century it was possible to roll a long ribbon of steel, 8 to 12 inches wide, in a continuous process. Manufacturers, especially automobile makers, wanted much wider sheets, but no way had been found to roll them on a continuous mill.

When wider sheets were attempted, they would sometimes slide off the rolls. It was then thought that the rolls should be even-surfaced cylinders, that is, until John Butler Tytus came along. He conceived the idea that the rolls should be slightly convex. If the rolls were convex, he argued, they would provide a guide for the sheet and prevent it from sliding off the rolls.

After graduating from Yale in 1897, young Tytus had returned to his home in Middletown, Ohio, and gone to work in his father's paper mill, which he was expected eventually to own and manage. But after a few years he became bored with his job and one day, out of curiosity, he wandered into a hand sheet mill of the American Rolling Mill Company. He watched with fascination the slow, hot, heavy work and counted twenty-two times that the sheets were handled. He concluded that a "business that had so much lost motion had plenty of future for a young man." He asked for a job. The superintendent, Charles R. Hook, who later became president of the company, did his best to discourage this rather frail-looking young gentleman. "It will break your back," he told Tytus.

"Perhaps," Tytus answered, "but I want to try it."

Young Tytus was hired as a spare hand, the lowliest job in the mill. Within eighteen months he was a skilled performer at every job in the plant, and in another year was appointed super-intendent of the company's hand sheet mill in Zanesville, Ohio. All the while he was thinking of ways to save "lost motion" in the hand mills. At his father's paper mill he had seen paper made in long sheets. This inspired him to make a pro-phetic remark to Hook, "Some day, Charlie, we'll be making sheets in long strips like they make paper."

Hook had faith in the ideas of his young employee and arranged to let him conduct experiments in an idle plant in Ashland, Kentucky. With one hundred workers, all pledged to secrecy, Tytus set out for Ashland. The years 1922 and 1923 were marked by some progress but also by many setbacks. But Hook's faith in Tytus never wavered, and he poured more money into the experiments. Finally, in 1924, Tytus put to-gether a wide-sheet mill with nineteen pairs of rolls that produced sheets up to 36 inches wide and as thin as 0.065 inch for the first time in the world.

The Tytus mill, however, was not fully continuous. By the time the steel had passed through the first fourteen pairs of rolls, it had cooled off so much that it had to be reheated. Then it was put through the last five finishing rolls. The great contribution of Tytus was the discovery that the rolls should be slightly convex to roll wide sheets.

The fully continuous wide hot-strip mill was developed by another company, and the best features of this mill and the Tytus mill were combined to make the modern continuous wide hot-strip mill. Within eight years about half a billion dollars had been invested in twenty-seven such mills.

Cold Rolling and Cold Reduction

In all the rolling mills discussed so far, the iron and steel were described as being at a red-hot rolling temperature, when they are soft enough to be shaped by the heavy pressure of the rolls. But steel in a cold condition—at ordinary room temperature—can also be rolled. Cold rolling imparts a very smooth, high polish to the surface of the steel.

The effects of cold rolling were discovered by accident. One day in 1859 a workman's tongs fell between moving rolls, and when they came out, they had a high polish. This led to the commercial development of cold rolling. Toward the end of the last century cold rolling was widely used to give a smooth, bright surface to thin strips of steel for clock springs and small articles of the hardware trade.

The primary purpose of cold reduction, on the other hand, is to reduce the thickness of steel in a cold condition. The steel is also made almost satiny smooth and highly lustrous. But cold reduction does more than reduce the thickness of steel and impart a smooth surface. It alters the internal structure of the steel so that after heat treatment it can be shaped cold in presses to a degree never before possible. When cold-reduced sheets first appeared, they differed so much from hot-rolled sheets that Charles Hook of the American Rolling Mill Company hailed them as an "entirely new product in the steel industry."

How was that so? The shaping of steel in stamping presses is known as drawing, that is, drawing out the steel. Hand-rolled sheets could be drawn, or shaped, in a cold condition only to a moderate degree. If an attempt were made to shape one, say, into the rounded form of an automobile fender of that period, the sheet would crack. A cold-reduced sheet, on the other hand, can be deep-drawn in a press to a remarkable degree. A large cold-reduced sheet will yield in a press to form the top of an automobile body, and a smaller sheet will curve into the shape of an automatic toaster. This was unthinkable before the introduction of cold reduction.

The continuous hot-strip mill and the cold-reduction mill should be thought of together. The first provided wide sheets of uniform high quality in mass quantities, and the second transformed them into an entirely new product. Both mills brought about an historic change in the economy and way of life in advanced industrial nations by opening up a whole new world of manufacturing possibilities—the mass production of consumer products made partly or wholly of steel sheets. Heading the list was the automobile, followed by a legion of home appliances and other products of everyday use.

The automobile is said to have provided millions of people with a house on wheels. It may also be claimed with equal truth that life in the home was revolutionized, thanks largely to the deep-drawing property of cold-reduced sheets.

In the 1920's most families hung a sign, "Ice," outside their homes when they wanted ice delivered. "A twenty-five cent piece," a housewife might call out to the iceman on a hot summer day. Inside, she steamed her laundry on the back of a coal range and washed it on a scrubbing board. She did her ironing with flatirons kept hot on the coal range.

Today, the mechanical refrigerator is in more wired homes than any other electric appliance. The scrubbing board has been replaced by the washing machine and the flatiron by the electric iron. These products are made mostly of steel sheets.

Sheets, of both carbon and alloy steels, have more uses than any other single steel product. A large portion of the food we eat, the dairy products we consume, the cotton cloth we wear or use in bed sheets, table linen, and so on, are processed through mechanized equipment in which sheet steel predominates. Machines plow the land, throw in the seed, cultivate and harvest the crops, milk cows, pasteurize and package the milk. It may be said that the machine mothers the crop from seed to the refrigerator, and the machine relies greatly on sheet steel.

Important other uses of sheets are in the electrical, drug, and chemical manufacturing industries, aircraft, passenger trains, ships, petroleum refining, surgical and medical equipment, furniture, office desks and other business equipment such as filing cabinets and business machines, restaurant facilities, sporting and camping goods, toys, and finally, in machinery of every description. Given a protective coating of zinc, which is called galvanizing, steel sheets are made into roofing and gutters, highway culverts, garbage pails, and ordinary water pails. Many tons of sheets are converted annually into tin plate for the preservation of food and for other uses, such as containers for paint, tobacco, and soft drinks.

It was the automobile that brought about the steel industry's greatest technological change in this century, measured in the degree that it directly affected the modern way of life. Sheet steel is the magic carpet on which we have ridden to new adventures in living.

12

New Processes, New Products

This chapter is devoted primarily to processes and products introduced after World War II, the most important of which is the basic oxygen converter steelmaking process. But first we will catch up on two important processes which originated earlier—the electric steelmaking process and the electrolytic tin-plating process.

The Electric Furnace

It was inevitable that men would one day think of applying the heat generated by electricity for metallurgical purposes. The idea was first given life in 1800 by an experiment of Sir Humphrey Davy in which he produced an electric arc between two carbon points, using an electric battery. A number of investigators were intrigued by the possibility of utilizing the current from a powerful electric battery to heat a small furnace, but their efforts met with only minor success. It was not until the 1880's when electricity became commercially available through the use of generators that the first electric furnaces of any practical importance appeared.

Various methods of using electrical energy to heat a furnace were tried, but the electric arc principle demonstrated by Sir Humphrey became the most successful. The electric arc produces intense heat. In 1886 the distinguished French metallurgist Dr. Paul Héroult in a laboratory experiment utilized an electric arc to produce metallic aluminum. He continued his researches with other metals in furnaces of his own design and in 1899 produced steel for the first time by the electric arc process.

What Héroult did was to insert two parallel carbon electrodes through the roof of his furnace, in the bottom of which was his charge of molten iron and scrap. A powerful electric current was turned on in both electrodes which were lowered until electric arcs leaped from the ends of the electrodes to the metal in the charge. The intense heat of the arcs refined the iron and scrap into steel. The Héroult-type furnace, with improvements, is the kind used for steelmaking today.

Steel was first produced by the electric arc process in the United States in 1906. Electric furnace production was given its initial strong impetus around 1911 by demands from the automobile industry for alloy steels. The electric furnace originally became identified only with the production of high-grade alloy steels, but it later was developed into a versatile instrument for the manufacture of a wide range of steels. More than half of its production is now carbon steel, but it still makes practically all of the stainless, tool, and other specialty steels used by the chemical, automotive, aviation, transportation, machine-tool, and food-processing industries. The operation of an electric furnace is described in Part III, Chapter 17.

The Electrolytic Process

The electrolytic tin-plating process represents a great advance in the manufacture of a widely used consumer product—tin plate. Tin-plating, from its earliest days, was done by immersing iron sheets in a bath of molten tin. This was called the hot-dip method. Although production methods had been improved through mechanization, there had been no change in the basic principle until the invention of the electrolytic process.

After some years of experimentation, the electrolytic process was introduced commercially by the United States Steel Corporation in 1937. At first production was on a small scale. Then World War II came along and created a crisis in tin supplies. The United States depended on nations that now comprise Malaysia and Indonesia for 92 per cent of its tin imports. After Japan entered the war, these imports were completely cut off. There was not enough tin on hand for both military and civilian needs. The shortage of tin became so critical that the United States government decided to use its remaining reserves for tin-plating cans to preserve food for its armed forces and those of its allies. There would have been practically no tin to spare for civilians, were it not for the electrolytic process.

The electrolytic process requires from 60 to 80 per cent less tin than the hot-dip method. Here was an opportunity to stretch out the dwindling reserves of tin. United States Steel suggested to the government that more electrolytic tinning mills be built and offered to share its knowledge of the process with other tin-plate manufacturers. The suggestion and offer were eagerly accepted. United States Steel built nine more

electrolytic tinning mills, and other companies built eighteen.
The twenty-seven mills saved enough tin so that the government could spare tin plate for civilians, though on a rationed
basis. By the end of the war electrolytic tin-plate production
amounted to one-third of total tin-plate output. Now almost all
tin plate is manufactured by the electrolytic process, which is
described in Part III, Chapter 17.

Ultrathin Tin Plate

A recent development in tin-plate manufacture is the production of what is termed ultrathin tin plate. The standard
thickness of steel for tin plate in the United States has been
0.0113 inch. Goaded on by competition from aluminum, glass,
and paper containers, and lured by the large market for canned
citrus juices, the steel industry set out to roll steel half as thick
as the standard product—down to 0.0060 to 0.0030 inch.

Ultrathin tin plate approaches the weight of aluminum in
cans, is superior in strength, and can be handled more easily
and economically than any substitute material.

Steel Foil

The steel industry has gone a step further and rolled steel
until it is only 2/1,000 (0.002) of an inch thick and can be
rolled even 50 per cent thinner. This very thin material is called
steel foil.

Most of the foil is tin-plated, but it is also sold as plain steel
foil. Steel foil has greater strength and resistance to heat and
moisture than any other packaging material of equal weight.
This exciting new steel product is expected to have extensive
use in the multibillion-dollar packaging business.

Some of steel foil's most promising markets are for products in which steel is not now being used. Among these are various throw-away type containers such as TV dinner trays, pie plates, and pouches for storing food or heating frozen foods in water.

Steel foil can be laminated—that is, made to adhere securely —to paper, cardboard, plastics, and other materials. Such combinations open up wide possibilities for a new type of lightweight container with the strength of steel and possessing the added advantage of resistance to puncture, moisture, and insects. These qualities are not provided by any other material of similar weight. Shipping boxes and bags are two examples of these new containers. The laminated foil can also be used as wrapping sheets. Steel foil can be lacquered and lithographed to make packages colorful and attractive.

Oxygen in Steelmaking

The most important advance in steelmaking since the invention of the electric arc furnace is the use of a jet of pure oxygen to refine iron into steel. The idea of using oxygen in iron and steelmaking is not new. Henry Bessemer in 1856 suggested the possibility of using oxygen-enriched air to refine iron into steel and actually took out patents for the use of oxygen as a refining agent, thus anticipating the new process by almost exactly a hundred years.

But the scarcity and high cost of pure oxygen discouraged interest in its use for many years. Since the 1920's it has become possible to produce oxygen in volume at low cost. This has led to widespread experimentation in the United States with oxygen in the blast furnace and in the electric and open hearth furnaces. An increasing number of open hearth shops are applying oxygen in normal operating practices.

It was in Europe that experiments were first conducted with

oxygen as the sole refining agent in steelmaking. The first commercial production took place in the towns of Linz and Donawitz, in Austria, in 1952, and the process became known as the L-D, or basic oxygen, process. Two years later an L-D converter was installed in Canada, followed shortly by another in the United States.

The advantages of the L-D process are its speed, its relatively low cost of installation and operation, and its ability to produce a wide range of high-quality steels, including carbon and alloy steels and even stainless steel. In the economics of steelmaking it is the overall cost of producing a ton of steel that matters. In this respect the basic oxygen process beats all the others. It can produce 300 tons of steel per hour, compared to 50 tons in an open hearth furnace. On this basis, one L-D converter can match the output of six open hearth furnaces. The difference in productive capacity will widen still more as L-D converters grow larger. The average capacity of oxygen converters per heat of steel throughout the world is 90 tons, but in the United States it is 155 tons, and this figure is expected to go still higher. The world's largest converters are two 300-ton-capacity furnaces in the United States.

Rapid Spread of the L-D Process

It is not surprising that the new steelmaking process is spreading rapidly around the world. The number of oxygen converters has increased from one in 1952 to 307 in twenty-nine nations in 1965, and the number of converters and the nations using them continues to rise. Annual capacity of basic oxygen converters in the United States was 26,000,000 tons in 1965. World capacity in the same year was 102,000,000 tons and is expected to climb to over 160,000,000 tons by 1968.

The basic oxygen process is not only being adopted in large

steel-producing regions—United States, Canada, Western Europe, Russia, and Japan—but is being eagerly welcomed by many smaller nations, some of which are producing steel for the first time. Among those which have installed oxygen converters are Bulgaria, Greece, Malaysia, Peru, Portugal, Tunisia, and Turkey. The L-D process appeals to such nations because it can be used to make steel on a small scale and also because of its economy of installation and operation.

The open hearth process that toppled the once-proud Bessemer from first place as a steel producer is expected to suffer the same fate at the hands of the basic oxygen converter. The open hearth process has been steadily losing ground to the new process. From what has been said of the advantages of the L-D process, the reasons are obvious. But too much has been invested in open hearth shops to dispense with them quickly. Some authorities predict that no new open hearth furnaces will be built in the United States. Judging by the rate the L-D process is growing, it is expected to surpass open hearth production by the mid-1970's. A description of a basic oxygen converter in action will be found in Part III, Chapter 17.

A Backward Glance at Steelmaking Processes

This is a good point at which to cast a backward glance at the steelmaking processes which we have examined so far. Table 2 tells the story. The years in the table were selected because of their significance in production trends. It will be observed that the positions of the Bessemer and open hearth processes have been almost reversed. Bessemer production skidded from 86 per cent of total steel output in 1875 to 0.5 per cent in 1965. Open hearth production rose from 2 per cent in 1875 to a record high of 92 per cent in 1940, only to slide down to 72 per cent in 1965.

The crucible process was the principal steelmaking method until the invention of the Bessemer process in the 1850's. High-quality steel, especially machine-tool steel, continued to be made by the crucible process well into this century. Crucible production reached its peak in 1916, due to the demands of World War I. But notice how it faded out after 1920, as the superior electric furnace gained a foothold.

In the miscellaneous column we say good-bye to the ancient cementation process and the puddling furnace, both of which held on determinedly into the present century with a final spurt to 16,000 tons in 1906. They even lasted until 1920 after which they flickered out.

The latest newcomer, the basic oxygen process, shot up from less than 1 per cent in 1955 to 17.5 per cent in 1965. It is expected to account for more than half of United States steel production in the early 1970's.

Refining Steel in a Vacuum

All the steel-refining processes described so far have been conducted in the presence of air. But the interaction of air with molten steel and also with the furnace lining produces certain compounds which may enter into the steel and contaminate it. What may not be injurious in steel for ordinary uses may be so in steels destined for the severest stress and high-temperature service. The three offenders which enter steel from the atmosphere are oxygen, nitrogen, and hydrogen. The worst culprit is hydrogen. Minute traces of this gas dissolved in steel—4 to 8 parts per million—may later cause microcracks which can lead to failure of a vital part when subjected to great stress at high temperature. Hydrogen, as well as oxygen and nitrogen, can be eliminated from steel by the vacuum process. Note that this process is not associated with producing steel but with refining steel already made.

TABLE 2

Production of Steel by Processes and Percentages of Total Steel Production in the United States: Selected Periods, 1875–1965

(thousands of net tons)

Years	Open Hearth		Bessemer		Crucible		Electric		Miscellaneous		Basic Oxygen		Total Steel Production
	Net Tons	% of Total	Net Tons	% of Total	Net Tons	% of Total	Net Tons	% of Total	Net Tons	% of Total	Net Tons	% of Total	Net Tons
1875	9	2.0	375	86.0	39	9	—	—	13	3.0	—	—	436
1890	575	11.0	4,130	86.0	80	2	—	—	4	1.0	—	—	4,790
1900	3,806	33.0	7,487	66.0	113	a	—	—	5	a	—	—	11,411
1906	12,298	47.0	13,749	53.0	142	a	—	—	16	a	—	—	26,205
1908	8,777	56.0	6,851	44.0	71	a	—	—	7	a	—	—	15,706
1909	16,233	61.0	10,450	39.0	120	a	16	a	10	a	—	—	26,830
1916	35,185	73.0	12,386	26.0	145	a	190	a	1	a	—	—	47,907
1920	36,593	77.0	9,949	21.0	81	a	562	1.0	4	a	—	—	47,189
1940	61,573	92.0	3,709	5.5	1	a	1,700	2.5	—	—	—	—	66,983
1950	86,263	89.0	4,535	4.7	—	—	6,038	6.3	—	—	—	—	96,836
1955	105,359	90.0	3,320	3.0	—	—	8,357	7.0	—	—	—	—	117,036
1957	101,658	90.0	2,475	2.0	—	—	8,582[b]	8.0	—	—	—	—	112,715
1958	75,879	89.0	1,396	2.0	—	—	7,980[b]	9.0	—	—	—	—	85,255
1959	81,669	87.5	1,380	1.4	—	—	8,532	9.1	—	—	1,864	2	93,446
1965	94,193	72.0	586	0.5	—	—	13,804	10.0	—	—	22,879	17.5	131,462

Source: American Iron and Steel Institute

[a] Less than 1 per cent

[b] Includes oxygen converter

Vacuum Melting

Refining steel by the agency of a vacuum was known and practiced early in the century, but it was not pushed because there was no great need for it. It was the jet engine, with its requirements for metals to operate at high stress and temperature, that led to vacuum melting on a commercial scale.

The steel to be vacuum-melted is already of high quality. It is generally made in the electric furnace, but open hearth steel may also be used. The solid section of steel to be melted is quite small. It is placed in a crucible in which a constant state of vacuum is maintained by powerful pumps. The crucible is surrounded by water-cooled copper tubing. A high-frequency alternating current is passed through the steel within the crucible. The resistance of the steel to the current creates the heat which melts the steel. The melted steel is in a constant state of agitation, thus exposing all parts of the metal to the pulling force of the vacuum, which literally sucks the gases out of the steel.

Vacuum Degassing, or Casting

The need to remove gases from large masses of steel, particularly from ingots to be forged into generator shafts and turbine rotors, led to the development of techniques for degassing steel fresh from the furnace. Vacuum degassing, or vacuum casting as the process is called, is being done on an increasing scale.

A ladle of molten steel, freshly tapped from the furnace, is placed over a tank in which a vacuum has been created. Directly beneath the tank is an ingot mold. By means of a stopper in a hole at the bottom of the ladle, the molten steel is allowed to pour a little at a time through the vacuum chamber into the ingot mold. In its passage through the vacuum cham-

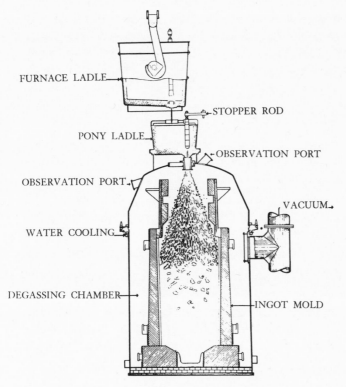

FURNACE LADLE

STOPPER ROD

PONY LADLE

OBSERVATION PORT

OBSERVATION PORT

VACUUM

WATER COOLING

DEGASSING CHAMBER

INGOT MOLD

Equipment to degass steel for extra large ingots. As molten steel pours through the degassing chamber it forms into droplets. The droplets are purified by the powerful vacuum pumps which suck out minute traces of harmful gases, chiefly hydrogen. The falling droplets slowly build up into an ingot. *American Iron and Steel Institute.*

ber, the liquid steel separates into droplets, thus exposing the maximum surface of the steel to the sucking action of the vacuum pumps and facilitating the withdrawal of the gases. As much as 9,600 cubic feet of gases may be withdrawn from a ton of steel. Some of the degassed ingots weigh as much as 250 tons.

Steels melted or cast in a vacuum are purer and stronger than those produced in the presence of air. They have improved mechanical properties at high temperature, greater ductility, and a high degree of uniformity in quality. These steels are the latest answer of the steel industry to the exacting requirements of supersonic planes and space vehicles. The electric industry now specifies vacuum-cast steel for all products subject to severe stress and high temperature.

Continuous Casting

Another important new process is not concerned with making steel but with shaping it. It is called continuous casting. It is significant because it strikingly illustrates the trend in the steel industry toward simplification of processes, aided by computer systems. The steel industry is characterized by what is known as the batch process of manufacture. One definition of batch is "a quantity of material produced at one operation." There is a long series of manufacturing steps taken in a steel plant from smelting the iron to producing finished steel products ready for sale. Steel is heavy and to move it from one step to another involves special handling equipment. All of these steps taken together consume considerable time and slow down production. Now certain steps in the production of semifinished steel products are being eliminated through continuous casting.

Here again we find Henry Bessemer ahead of his time. In 1860 he conceived of casting molten steel continuously into steel plates, but the method he proposed was, and is, impractical. But he had the vision to foresee the possibility. Continuous casting offered such promising advantages in speed and labor-saving that the idea was not abandoned. Experiments led to success in the continuous casting of nonferrous metals, but

early attempts with steel failed or were only partially successful. But in recent years success has finally been achieved in
continuously casting semifinished steel such as blooms, slabs,
and billets. These constitute the basic stock for making finished
steel products.

Blooms are large, chunky steel sections, suitable for rolling
into rails and structural shapes such as girders for bridges and
buildings. Slabs are wider and flatter than blooms and are
rolled into flat products such as plate and sheet. Billets are long,
narrow sections of steel. They are the stock from which bars,
rods, pipes, and tubes are derived.

Production of blooms, slabs, and billets by present methods involves five steps: (1) Preparing the ingot molds in a
foundry, (2) pouring steel from the furnace into the molds,
where it cools and solidifies into ingots, the first solid form in
which most steel is made, (3) stripping, or lifting the molds
from the ingots which have meanwhile cooled down too much
for rolling, (4) reheating the ingots in a special furnace to
rolling temperature, and (5) rolling the ingots into blooms and
slabs, and the blooms, in turn, into billets, on appropriate
rolling mills.

Continuous casting eliminates these steps and casts molten
steel fresh from the furnace directly into semifinished forms.
The equipment used in continuous casting varies somewhat,
but the basic principle is always the same. One type of machine
employed for the production of billets will be described here.

A ladle of molten steel is lifted to the top of a tall, vertical
structure and placed in position. The reason for the elevation
and the vertical structure is to allow the molten steel to flow
downward. A hole in the bottom of the ladle is opened, and
the steel flows into a receptacle which serves as a reservoir.
From the reservoir the steel passes into a long, vertical mold
directly beneath it. The mold is made of copper and is water-
cooled.

On entering the mold, the steel is chilled and a hard outer shell is formed, from ¼ to ½ inch thick. The outwardly hardened casting continues through the mold, and as it emerges it is gripped by rollers which pull it on downward. Still gripped by the rollers, the casting is passed through a water spray which does most of the cooling. After the casting has completely solidified, it is cut into lengths by oxyacetylene torches.

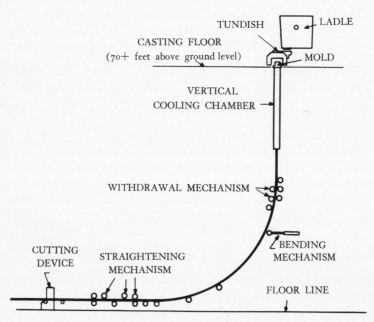

The diagram represents one type of machine used in the continuous casting of steel billets. The elevation of the ladle permits molten steel to flow down into the mold, or cooling chamber, where the hard shell of a casting is formed. Gripped by rollers, the casting is pulled downward and passes through a water spray, not represented here. *United States Steel Corporation.*

Continuous casting of semifinished steel represents a major breakthrough in shaping steel. Adoption of the new technology has been going on for some years in major steel centers throughout the world. Most of those in use are in Western Europe, with the remainder in Russia, Japan, Canada, and Mexico. After a slow start, continuous casting is ' undergoing an explosive growth in the United States, where it is expected that thirty-six machines will be in use by 1968.

Major Breakthrough in Shaping Steel

The effects of continuous casting on steel mill operations and employment are at present impossible to estimate. But the reduction in manpower will be considerable. In less than one hour, molten steel can be transformed into semifinished steel products, compared to many hours, more frequently days, required in the steps mentioned above. Owing to the savings in time, labor, and fuel, the new process can produce semifinished steel at lower cost. Moreover, the steel is of generally higher quality than semifinished steel produced by conventional methods. Continuously cast steel has a better surface and internal structure than steel solidified in an ingot mold. Greater uniformity of quality can be attained through the use of electronic controls.

13

Automation

Ever since man invented the wheel some 5,000 years ago, automation was bound to come someday. From the wheel came the machine. Once man had a machine in his hands, he couldn't let it alone. He made it more powerful, more productive, more complex, and capable of performing a greater variety of jobs. Now it has a memory and can correct its own mistakes.

Automation, in the sense of automatic machinery, is not new. To go back no further than 1795, Oliver Evans built an automatic grist mill in Philadelphia. In his own words, it performed "every necessary movement of the grain and meal, from one part of the mill to another . . . through all the various operations, from the time the grain is emptied from the wagoner's bag . . . until it is completely manufactured into

flour . . . ready for packing into barrels, for sale or exporta-
tion. All of which is performed by the force of water, without
the aid of manual labor, except to set the different machines in
motion."

Henry Bessemer built a factory for which he designed what
he described as "self-acting machinery," capable of doing the
work of eighty to ninety men, and which could operate "without a skilled attendant" and "throw itself out of gear when its
task was completed."

Automation in the Steel Industry

Automation, as commonly understood today, is distinguished from earlier automatic machinery chiefly by use of the
electronic computer. Automation, in this modern sense, is
moving rapidly into the steel industry, and its pace can be
expected to quicken in the years ahead. Some continuous hot-
strip mills are completely automated. Computers on a mill
enable it to take the temperature of the passing ribbon of steel,
compute the space between the rolls and correct any variations
in the thickness of the steel as it races along. At the end of the
line, a ticket is printed identifying the weight, dimensions, and
other characteristics of the steel. As a result, the speed and
accuracy of the mill have been raised to new levels.

Applied to the blast furnace, computer systems automatically
select, transport, and charge raw materials into the furnace.
Computers control the flow, pressure, and character of the
blast. Automatic sensing devices constantly measure the chemical constituents of the gases discharged from the top of the
furnace. In another ten years the blast furnace may be completely automated.

At some steel plants computers regulate, to a greater or lesser
degree, the power plants, electric furnace, basic oxygen fur-

nace, sintering plant, annealing lines, and certain other hot-rolling mills in addition to the hot-strip mill. Computers also control galvanizing and tin-plating lines and other miscellaneous equipment.

The steel industry is being automated in a step-by-step process. Each stage of operation is being automated separately. Gradually, these will be linked together in area computer systems, and these, in turn, will be linked to master computer systems for an entire plant. Administration of the business— sales, accounting, production planning, research, and so on— will be tied in with all the plants of a company in an overall integrated system. Orders and information will pulsate back and forth continuously between administrative nerve centers, sales offices, mines, and plants.

Customers will enjoy a speed of service and quality of products never before experienced. Operators in the mills will serve as monitors to observe any abnormality in the flow of operations. Assisting them will be maintenance crews trained to keep the system working smoothly. Both groups will have to be of a high order of intelligence and technical training.

The Displaced Steelworker

In a statement on automation, the United Steelworkers of America, the union representing most steelworkers, said "It is not our objective to obstruct the introduction of new technology." But the union is deeply troubled by the displacement of its members now taking place and the outlook for even greater displacement in the future. "Automation," the union said in a resolution, "must not be allowed to develop into a headless monster destroying more than it creates."

American steel companies, on their part, are aware of their responsibility toward employees affected by technological change and have worked out programs with the union to deal with the problems involved. The programs vary somewhat from company to company. The following procedure is being followed by one large steel company.

As soon as plans are completed to modernize equipment, which generally means automation, an analysis is made of the number of employees to be affected. Their length of service, age, family status, place of residence, seniority status, and ability to perform other work is determined.

Their eligibility for pension, severance pay, and unemployment compensation is also determined. The job openings on the new equipment are also considered.

A study is then made of what steps may be taken to continue employment of the affected workers, by finding them jobs elsewhere in the plant, in other company plants in the same area, with other employers, or through the local state employment office. Consideration is also given to retraining employees for work on the new equipment, or providing them with on-the-job training for other openings in the plant.

Notices of the change are sent to the union, to the affected employees, and to the general public. At the appropriate time, interviews are held with the affected employees, at which they are informed of other job prospects and of their rights regarding pension, vacations, insurance coverage, severance pay, and other provisions. Each employee decides which of the available choices he prefers.

The degree of success attained through this procedure varies with each case of technological change. Some cases are 100 per cent successful, and others are only partly so. In one instance, when an old rolling mill was replaced by an automated mill, 1,346 employees were affected. A survey made several years later showed that 953 employees, or 71 per cent, after being retrained, were working in the new mill. Another 109, or 8 per cent, were working in other departments of the plant. There was one actual layoff, whereas 29 were on sick leave. The remaining 254 employees chose retirement, or preferred to leave the company, died, or took a leave of absence.

In another plant of the same company, the changeover was not so successful. Of 1,373 employees involved, 492 were found jobs in that plant or other plants of the company, 293 retired on pension, 282 chose severance pay and left the company, and 306 had to be laid off.

Higher Education Needed

Modern technology is moving us into a new world where the accent is on education. Steelworkers once boasted of their muscles, but no more. With the advent of automation, the shift is from brawn to brains. In the steel industry this means higher requirements in education and a decrease in the proportion of blue collar workers and an increase in the proportion of white collar workers.

Speaking in this connection, the president of one steel company said, "I would put first the desirability of more and better education—for our school children and for the people currently employed. Workers in all categories will need greater effectiveness with the tools of communication and analysis. They will need broader knowledge and broader understanding."

One of the problems encountered in retraining employees for jobs in automated steel mills is not so much their lack of work skills as inadequate basic education. When one steel company installed a continuous galvanizing line, qualifications for the new jobs required the ability to speak, read, and write English, and to do simple arithmetic problems. This was the first time in the company's history that an employee had to pass such tests to hold a job. Fully 20 per cent of the men employed on the old equipment were ineligible for the new jobs because they could not meet these basic qualifications.

Production workers are not the only ones feeling the pressure for better education. White collar workers and management personnel need broader knowledge and technical training to deal with and solve the problems arising from the increasingly complex technology of steelmaking. When the continuous galvanizing line, mentioned above, was installed, the number of white collar workers and supervisors increased almost 80 per cent. Within ten years, the upgrading of jobs resulted in 73 per cent higher wages than on the older equipment.

Some steel companies conduct educational programs especially designed to help employees adapt themselves to technological changes, particularly automation. The programs are open to all employees. In some cases the courses are arranged with universities. In one plant of a large steel company, over five hundred men graduated from a two-year college course.

Needed—More Education

The steel industry, like many other industries, is being transformed by the technological revolution now under way. The men who are losing out are generally those who, for one reason or another, cannot keep in step with the new technology. It does not mean that persons left on the wayside by technological change necessarily face long idleness or permanent unemployment. The Council of Economic Advisers to the President said in its 1964 report, "The worker made permanently unemployable by technological change is relatively rare," but added that the displaced worker may have to accept "a less challenging and lower paying job."

14

The Revolution of Rising Expectations

The machine is not the prerogative—the special privilege—of any nation. The machine civilization had its origin in the Industrial Revolution, when machinery began to replace manual labor around 1800. Water power drove the first machines. Then came steam, electricity, and petroleum fuels, and now we are beginning to use the atom.

The Industrial Revolution is still going on. It has barely reached some nations, and there are vast areas in Africa, Asia, and South America where it has not yet penetrated. Formerly, the Industrial Revolution rippled out slowly from its centers in Europe and the United States, but now it is spreading faster and will pick up speed in the years ahead.

The Machine Means Steel

The machine means steel, whether the machine is used to mine cobalt in the Republic of the Congo or to run a tractor in a nation trying to mechanize its agriculture. That is why people in many developing countries, striving to take their first steps toward industrialization, are fired with ambition to manufacture steel for part or all of their needs. This applies chiefly to countries which have one or more of the necessary raw materials and can import the others. Those with no raw materials have to import pig iron or scrap to convert into steel.

Before World War II thirty nations made steel. Every year since, others have joined the ranks and in 1965 the number reached sixty-one. Among the newcomers since the war are Argentina, Chile, Colombia, Puerto Rico, Peru, Uruguay, Cuba, Denmark, Ireland, Greece, Switzerland, Algeria, Egypt, Israel, Rhodesia, Taiwan, Burma, Ghana, Uganda, Pakistan, South Korea, Philippines, and Bulgaria. Some of the new steel producers, particularly those in the western world, already possess some industries, but they want to further their industrialization by establishing their own steel industry.

Steel is the economic underpinning of a machine economy. Over 95 per cent of civilization's metal requirements are met by steel. The consumption of steel per capita in a nation provides a key to a nation's living standards. This may be seen in Table 3, which gives the per capita consumption of steel in selected countries in 1959 and 1964. Steel consumption per capita is figured by adding the amount of steel produced and imported, then subtracting the amount exported, and dividing the remainder by the population figure.

Table 3 contains a number of surprises. For many years the United States enjoyed a fairly comfortable lead as the world's largest consumer of steel per person, but in 1959 Sweden began

TABLE 3

CONSUMPTION OF STEEL PER CAPITA IN SELECTED COUNTRIES, 1959 AND 1964

(in pounds per person)

COUNTRY	1959	1964	Increase or decrease of consumption per person, 1964 over 1959
North America			
United States	1,078	1,353	275
Canada	777	979	202
Latin America			
Argentina	213	205	—8
Brazil	81	95	14
Chile	130	163	33
Colombia	42	77	35
Mexico	82	143	62
Venezuela	231	262	31
Europe			
Western Europe			
Austria	458	596	138
Belgium-Luxembourg	616	922	306
Denmark	521	737	216
Finland	414	561	147
France	561	783	222
Greece	73	185	112
Ireland	106	178	72

TABLE 3 *(continued)*

COUNTRY	1959	1964	Increase or decrease of consumption per person, 1964 over 1959
Italy	312	486	174
Netherlands	524	719	195
Norway	550	697	147
Portugal	92	132	40
Spain	154	239	86
Sweden	997	1,371	374
Switzerland	559	799	240
Turkey	31	57	26
United Kingdom	730	964	234
West Germany	977	1,274	297
Yugoslavia	172	266	94

Socialist countries of Eastern Europe

Bulgaria	165	273	108
Czechoslovakia	964	1,096	132
East Germany	706	933	227
Hungary	383	493	110
Poland	429	563	134
Rumania	249	471	222
U.S.S.R.	607	781	174

Africa

Republic of South Africa	253	381	128

TABLE 3 *(continued)*

COUNTRY	1959	1964	Increase or decrease of consumption per person, 1964 over 1959
Far East			
China (mainland)	46	40	—6
India	18	35	17
Japan	359	713	354
Oceania			
Australia	693	944	250
New Zealand	370	513	143
Average of countries listed	394	537	

SOURCE: *The European Steel Market in 1964,* United Nations

edging up and in 1964 was in first place, with the United States in second position. Another surprise is to find Czechoslovakia in fourth place, ahead of such steel-producing areas as the United Kingdom, Canada, and France. The lowest consumption rate was in India.

It will be seen that the average consumption of steel per person in the forty countries listed rose from 394 to 537 pounds in the period covered. Argentina and mainland China were the only nations to show a decrease in per capita steel consumption. The largest gains were registered by Japan, Sweden, Belgium-Luxembourg, West Germany, and the United States, in that order.

Explosion in Steel Production

Accompanying the world's population explosion, there has been an explosion in world steel production, which has more than tripled between 1948 and 1965, rising from 165,800,000 to 501,407,000 tons. It is expected that by 1970 world steel production may rise to 570,000,000 tons.

Table 4 gives steel production by various countries of the world in 1965. The United States is the world's largest steel producer, a position it has held unchallenged since 1889, but Russia is becoming a close second. Still far behind both nations are Japan, West Germany, and the United Kingdom, which follow in that order.

World Iron Ore Reserves

As large steel-producing nations increase their output and as other nations become steel producers, the question arises: Will there be enough iron ore to sustain a growing world steel industry? The answer is Yes. Iron is the fourth most common element and the second most abundant metal in the earth's crust, of which it constitutes about 5 per cent. The core of the earth is believed to consist of iron and nickel, making iron the most plentiful element in the earth as a whole. Iron ores exist in great abundance near the earth's crust throughout the world. Known reserves are sufficient to meet all foreseeable needs for over 150 years, in spite of the fact that consumption is expected to more than double within the next 30 years. In addition, there are almost limitless amounts of iron-bearing materials, unusable now, which will become available as new mining and steelmaking techniques are perfected and transportation costs are reduced.

TABLE 4

1965 WORLD PRODUCTION OF STEEL BY COUNTRIES

(*thousands of short tons*)

North America		West Germany	40,586
United States	131,462	Italy	13,930
(U.S. % of		Netherlands	3,437
world)	(26.2%)	Total ECSC	94,715
Canada	10,024		
Total	141,486	*Other Western Europe*	
		Austria	3,552
Latin America		Denmark	452
Argentina	1,485	Finland	381
Brazil	3,219	Greece	235
Chile	470	Ireland	22
Colombia	268	Norway	756
Cuba	50	Portugal	303
Mexico	2,685	Spain	3,810
Peru	102	Sweden	5,208
Venezuela	658	Switzerland	395
Puerto Rico and		Turkey	651
Uruguay	55	United Kingdom	30,247
Total	8,992	Yugoslavia	1,940
		Total other	
Europe		Western	
Western Europe ECSC*		Europe	47,952
Belgium-		Total Western	
Luxembourg	15,153	Europe	142,667
France	21,609		

TABLE 4 *(continued)*

Socialist countries of Eastern Europe		*Middle East*	
		Egypt	200
Bulgaria	634	Israel	72
Czechoslovakia	9,480	Lebanon	20
East Germany	4,288	Total	292
Hungary	2,712	*Far East*	
Poland	10,013	India	6,899
Rumania	3,770	Japan	45,383
U.S.S.R.	100,305	Pakistan	13
		South Korea	143
Total Eastern Europe	131,202	Taiwan	275
Total Europe	273,869	Burma, Hong Kong, Malaysia, and Thailand	151
Africa		China (mainland)	13,228
Rhodesia	113	North Korea	1,150
Republic of South Africa	3,450	Total	67,242
Algeria, Ghana, Nigeria, and Uganda	77	*Oceania*	
		Australia	5,736
Total	3,640	New Zealand	50
		Philippines	100
		Total	5,886
		Total World	501,407

* European Coal and Steel Community

SOURCE: *American Iron and Steel Institute*

The principal iron ore resources of the world may be seen in
Table 5, which gives both explored and potential reserves in
each nation. Since iron ores vary in iron content, it is more
accurate to measure reserves as "iron-in-ore," which means the
amount of iron they are supposed to contain. A direct-shipping
ore is a natural ore that may be used pretty much as it comes
from the mine. A concentrating ore is a low-grade ore that may
be beneficiated into a concentrate. Explored reserves are those
that have been proven or measured by drilling or other techniques, so that their quantity and quality are known with
reasonable certainty. Potential resources include reserves that
are believed to exist on the basis of geological evidence but
which have not been thoroughly explored.

It will be seen in Table 5 that the world's largest reserves are
in the U.S.S.R., with nearly 15 billion tons of total resources.
Brazil bulks large in second place with over 10 billion tons,
whereas India is a very close third. The United States is in
fourth position, followed by China, Canada, and France, in
that order.

Altered Position of the United States

If we look back less than twenty years, the changes that have
taken place in the American iron ore industry and the steel
industry are almost incredible. The United States, the world's
largest steel producer, which made about half of the world's
steel less than a score of years ago, now accounts for little more
than one-fourth. The United States once imported little steel
and exported a great deal. Now the situation is reversed and
imports are almost four times as great as exports. The United
States, with the fourth largest iron ore reserves and once the
foremost ore producer, is now second to the Soviet Union and
actually imports more iron ore than it exports. Here, too, the

reverse was the case for many years. But following World War II, imports rose to several million tons a year and then began to soar, to 45,000,000 tons in 1965, compared to exports of only 7,000,000 tons.

To understand the present iron ore situation in the United States it is necessary to go back many years. Since the start of mining in the Lake Superior district in 1855, more than 3⅓ billion tons of iron ore have been taken from it. These were natural, direct-shipping ores, and represented the cream of the region, averaging 50 per cent or more in iron content. About 740,000,000 tons of these natural ores still remain, with an iron content above 45 per cent. If the United States relied on them for 80 per cent of its iron ore needs, as in the past, these ores would not last very long—not at the increasing rate of consumption, which will probably reach 235,000,000 tons a year by 1980.

Two-Point Program

But the steel industry of the United States has no intention of depleting these ores. For one thing, it is prudent to retain these reserves for any possible future emergency. The steel industry must plan far ahead. To assure itself of adequate supplies of iron ore and in the interest of national security, it has undertaken a two-point program to obtain iron ore from other sources. One source is foreign mines and the other is beneficiated low-grade ores, of which billions of tons exist in the Lake Superior region.

1. Foreign Iron Ores

Following World War II, private industry made an intensive search in other countries for large deposits of iron ore. Sources were discovered and developed in Ontario and the Quebec-Labrador region of Canada, in Venezuela, Peru, Chile, and several countries in West Africa, notably Liberia, Guinea, and Gabon. Except for the Quebec-Labrador region, most of these foreign mines yield high-quality natural ores which can be used directly in the blast furnace, except for some possible "agglomeration," which will be described in this chapter.

2. Billions of Tons of Low-Grade Ores

The low-grade ores of the Lake Superior district are hard, rocklike mixtures of iron oxides with silica. They are generally referred to as taconites and jaspers, and contain from 25 to 35 per cent iron. The iron oxides in some are magnetic and in others are nonmagnetic. After many years of research, methods have been developed to form concentrates of these ores, in which the iron content ranges from 62 to 67 per cent. All methods require that the ore first be ground to a fine powder in order to separate the iron oxide grains from the waste material known as silica. The iron oxide particles in magnetic taconite are separated from the silica particles by magnetic attraction. Nonmagnetic iron oxides in other taconites and jaspers are treated by other, more complex processes.

Low-grade iron ores in other parts of the United States—Alabama, Texas, Utah, Colorado, and Wyoming—are also being beneficiated.

Agglomeration

Concentrates of low-grade ores, and most of the imported ores, are too fine to be used in the blast furnace. Iron ore should have a certain "bulk" and strength, which coarser ores have. To get around the difficulty, the fine ores are agglomerated.

One definition of agglomerate is "to gather in a ball or mass." Iron ores are agglomerated into sinter, pellets, nodules, and briquettes. In sintering, iron ore is mixed with a pulverized fuel such as coke or coal and the mixture is placed on a grate and burned under forced draft to a hard, porous mass called sinter.

Agglomerates have the proper firmness and are of the right size for the blast furnace. These physical properties combined with their high iron content make them an excellent raw material for iron smelting. Agglomerated concentrates of taconites and jaspers of the Lake Superior region are now preferred to its existing natural ores. Iron ores are being increasingly agglomerated in other steel-producing nations.

Effect of the Program on Ore Imports

The chief steel centers of the United States grew up along or near the southern shores of the Great Lakes, to be accessible to iron ores shipped down from the Lake Superior district. Ores were transported as far south as the great steel city of Pittsburgh. These steel centers in Illinois, Indiana, Ohio, New York, Michigan, and Pennsylvania make 75 per cent of the steel produced in the United States.

After World War II there was considerable expansion in the American steel industry, and much of it took place away from these areas—on the eastern, western, and Gulf coasts, and in the western interior. These new mills were too far from the Lake Superior district to receive their ore from there because of high transportation costs, which are a very important factor in determining the cost of ore. The new mills either had to use rather inadequate local ores or import ores, and they chose to do the latter. New, large, specially designed, ocean-going ships made possible greatly reduced freight charges. In many instances, it cost no more to transport ore 2,000 miles from a

TABLE 5
WORLD IRON ORE RESOURCES
Iron-in-Ore
(millions of metric tons)
Geologically Explored Reserves

	Direct-Shipping Ore	Concentrating Ore	Total Explored	Potential Resources	Total
North America					
Canada	195.2	1,558.4	1,753.6	2,812.8	4,566.4
United States	269.9	2,284.3	2,554.2	6,042.2	8,596.4
Total	465.1	3,842.7	4,307.8	8,855.0	13,162.8
Central America					
Honduras	—	—	—	4.2	4.2
Mexico	60.0	—	60.0	89.7	149.7
Total	60.0	—	60.0	93.9	153.9
South America					
Argentina	—	47.5	47.5	36.5	84.0
Brazil	1,737.0	60.0	1,797.0	8,487.5	10,284.5

Chile	119.9	—	119.9	167.1	287.0
Colombia	24.0	—	24.0	24.0	48.0
Peru	25.7	275.0	300.7	31.4	332.1
Venezuela	622.7	—	622.7	316.5	939.2
Total	2,529.3	382.5	2,911.9	9,063.0	11,974.8
Europe					
Austria	—	37.2	37.2	78.1	115.3
Bulgaria	12.6	81.7	94.3	—	94.3
Czechoslovakia	—	24.3	24.3	54.3	78.6
Finland	—	87.5	87.5	64.0	151.5
France	1,924.0	257.8	2,181.8	1,880.0	4,061.8
Germany (East)	—	11.5	11.5	—	11.5
Germany (West)	19.8	425.9	445.7	1,021.6	1,467.3
Greece	—	38.6	38.6	41.4	80.0
Hungary	—	4.8	4.8	4.8	9.6
Italy	5.7	12.1	17.8	20.7	38.5
Luxembourg	—	60.0	60.0	21.0	81.0
Norway	5.4	73.9	79.3	428.8	504.1
Poland	—	91.1	91.1	92.5	183.6

TABLE 5 (continued)

	Direct-Shipping Ore	Concentrating Ore	Total Explored	Potential Resources	Total
Rumania	17.2	—	17.2	36.0	53.2
Spain	422.5	—	422.5	155.2	577.7
Sweden	1,164.8	228.5	1,393.3	507.9	1,901.2
Switzerland	—	10.0	10.0	9.5	19.5
United Kingdom	675.8	—	675.8	325.3	1,001.1
U.S.S.R.	1,549.7	7,696.3	9,246.0	5,571.2	14,817.2
Yugoslavia	11.9	71.1	83.0	7.4	90.4
Total	5,809.4	9,212.3	15,021.7	10,315.7	25,337.4
Asia					
Burma	—	16.7	16.7	—	16.7
China (mainland)	482.2	947.7	1,375.9	3,303.3	4,679.2
Hong Kong	—	3.6	3.6	—	3.6
India	3,360.0	33.6	3,393.6	6,555.0	9,948.6
Indochina	24.7	—	24.7	42.0	66.7
Indonesia	1.4	—	1.4	6.2	7.6
Iran	—	—	—	34.2	34.2

Israel	—	1.8	1.8	3.5	5.3
Japan	5.1	18.8	23.9	—	23.9
Korea	—	167.3	167.3	260.0	427.3
Malaysia	—	28.8	28.8	—	28.8
Thailand	—	—	—	12.6	12.6
Turkey	24.6	—	24.6	11.7	36.3
Total	3,844.0	1,218.3	5,062.3	10,228.5	15,290.8
Oceania					
Australia	255.6	45.0	300.6	907.1	1,207.7
Philippines	4.7	14.4	19.1	—	19.1
Total	260.3	59.4	319.7	907.1	1,226.8
Africa					
Algeria	75.8	—	75.8	—	75.8
Angola	98.4	—	98.4	98.4	196.8
Egypt	7.5	—	7.5	75.0	82.5
French Cameroons	—	40.0	40.0	—	40.0
Gabon	—	63.4	63.4	315.0	378.4
Guinea	260.0	—	260.0	1,170.0	1,430.0

TABLE 5 (continued)

	Direct-Shipping Ore	Concentrating Ore	Total Explored	Potential Resources	Total
Ivory Coast	—	—	—	130.0	130.0
Liberia	6.6	46.6	53.2	290.0	343.2
Mauritania	95.3	—	95.3	—	95.3
Morocco	13.8	22.1	35.9	56.2	92.1
Zambia & Malawi	126.0	—	126.0	—	126.0
Sierra Leone	—	152.6	152.6	—	152.6
Republic of South Africa	270.5	36.5	307.0	488.0	795.0
Swaziland	32.2	—	32.2	32.1	64.3
Tunisia	9.9	0.6	10.5	11.0	21.5
Total	996.0	361.8	1,357.8	2,665.7	4,023.5
WORLD TOTAL	13,964.1	15,077.0	29,041.1	42,128.9	71,170.0

SOURCE: "Iron-Ore Resources of the World," by R. W. Hyde, D. M. Lane, and W. W. Glaser (Arthur D. Little, Inc.). *Engineering and Mining Journal*, 163, No. 12, Dec. 1962, pp. 84–88. (This is the latest report available as of 1967.)

foreign mine than a much shorter distance from an American mine. The result is that seaboard steel mills can buy foreign ore as cheap as or more cheaply than local ores, and much more cheaply than Lake Superior ores.

This migration of steel plants to seaboard sites was done intentionally to utilize high-quality ores from newly developed foreign mines. Another purpose was to be in a better competitive position over inland plants to export steel and sell it in the surrounding markets, where population and industries were growing rapidly. In other words, it was increasingly recognized that the rich, natural ores of Lake Superior were facing depletion, and farsighted companies realized that they would have to depend more and more on foreign ores and acted accordingly.

However, the Lake Superior district has a bright future in beneficiated low-grade ores, which will eventually replace natural ores in the Midwest steel areas mentioned above.

There is another important reason why steel companies have turned increasingly to foreign ores. This is the rising costs of iron and steelmaking. As steel production expanded, the demand for smelted iron rose in proportion. Instead of spending money to build more blast furnaces, efforts were made to raise the output of existing furnaces. This was done partly by using higher quality iron ores. Since many foreign ores are of better quality than American ores, the former were preferred by furnace operators. Consequently, there has been a marked rise in ore imports for steel mills in coastal areas, and even inland mills at Pittsburgh, and in Alabama and Texas.

At the same time, research was intensified to raise blast furnace efficiency by other means. Numerous metallurgical and technological improvements were realized which, combined with high-quality ores, have at least doubled the production rate of the blast furnace.

Summing Up

It was the availability of high-quality foreign iron ores to areas where the American steel industry was expanding most that was largely responsible for the spectacular rise in imports since World War II—from roughly 3 per cent to 32 per cent of total national consumption. It is predicted that by 1975 the United States will be importing 40 per cent of its iron ore.

Newly developed iron ore resources in Africa, South America, and Canada will have an effect on international iron ore trade. Some of the new mines can as easily ship ore to other markets as to the United States. Canadian ores can go east to Europe. West Africa is about the same distance from European consuming centers as from the United States. Venezuelan ore can cross the Atlantic to Europe, whereas ore from the west coast of South America can go all the way to Japan.

It is evident, from what has been said here, that there will be no future shortage of iron ore for the steel needs of the world, as the machine civilization spreads around the earth, fulfilling the "revolution of rising expectations."

15

Steel in the Atomic-Space Age

The materials at man's command in any given period of civilization have put a limit to his advances in technology. He could progress just so far with stone, copper, and bronze in their respective ages.

Iron offered much wider possibilities. Its uses were greatly multiplied in all branches of life. There seemed to be no limit to what could be done with this adaptable metal, and new uses merely waited on man's inventiveness.

Finally, one invention, steam power, heralded the end of the Iron Age. Steam power not only terminated the 3,500-year reign of iron but also marked the beginning of a new, important stage in metallurgy that is still with us. For the first time in history man faced the critical problem of finding a material to contain the intense heat he was capable of creating. He still faces that problem today.

While it is true that some of the new technologies that came in with the Steel Age—automobiles, aircraft, chemical manufacturing—called for harder, longer-wearing, corrosion-resistant steels, the metallurgist was able to meet these demands through the development of various alloy steels. But the problem of heat constantly challenged him and was never satisfactorily solved.

The steam engine itself did not present formidable problems, but what followed it did—steam and gas turbines, introduced early in the twentieth century for the generation of electricity. The designers of turbines became the metallurgist's severest taskmaster, demanding a metal that could hold its strength at ever higher temperatures in order to realize greater thermal efficiency. No sooner did the metallurgist meet one demand than he was presented with a stiffer requirement. The history of high temperature alloy steels and steam and gas turbines went hand in hand. The blades of a turbine are subjected not only to high temperatures but also to tremendous stress. They are also exposed to severe corrosive conditions. Engineers say that they could double the efficiency of the gas turbine if a metal could be found to stand up under these conditions for a prolonged period at temperatures above 1,800° F.

The turbine is the first mechanism for which technological advance has been held up for want of a suitable material. When we turn to nuclear reactors, supersonic planes, and rockets, we find that alloy steels are overtaxed in some critical applications.

At the threshold of the Atomic-Space Age, technology has outdistanced metallurgy. Man can generate heat beyond the capacity of any known material to contain it. Engineers have designs on their drafting boards that call for metals of greater strength and heat resistance than any available. Much progress has been made and more can be expected to follow in the scientific and technological revolution now under way.

The Problems of Strength and Extreme Temperatures

Strength and the capacity to withstand extremely high temperatures—these are the two chief properties space engineers seek in materials. The ability to withstand very low temperatures is also important, but much less so than high ones.

The first essential of any flying vehicle, from a propeller plane to a spacecraft, is to be as light as possible while still possessing sufficient strength to withstand the thrust of its power and the aerodynamic forces exerted on its frame and surfaces. The strength of a metal in relation to its weight is spoken of as its strength-to-weight ratio. The higher the ratio, the less of a metal is required for a given purpose. Consequently, the designers of supersonic aircraft and space vehicles stress their need for metals with higher strength-to-weight ratios.

When a metallurgist refers to the heat resistance of a metal, he means the maximum temperature at which it can still function in an engine or serve, say, on the wing of a plane, without softening and losing its usefulness. When a supersonic plane or space vehicle plunges through the atmosphere, it is exposed to extremely high temperatures for a relatively short time. A metal that cannot withstand intense heat for a prolonged period may be able to absorb it for a time measured in minutes. You can pass your hand safely through the heat above a flame that you could not endure, holding still, even for seconds. When the X-15 rocket plane dives back through the atmosphere, its metal skin glows red with heat, but the exposure to high temperature is so brief—only eleven minutes—that any softening of the metal surface is not damaging.

The metals in containers of liquefied gases, chiefly hydrogen and oxygen, used to power rockets and spacecraft must be able to withstand low temperatures. These fuels, stored under pres-

sure at temperatures that go below $-400°$ F, are highly corrosive, especially under stress. Stainless steel, which meets the
conditions of pressure, temperature, and corrosion extremely
well, is often used in these containers. The temperature on the
outer surface of a spacecraft during hours of darkness is only
about $-32°$ F.

Steel for the Space Age

A plane or space vehicle, like an automobile, is composed of
many materials, each chosen for the application to which it is
best suited. Alloy steels, superalloys, and the alloys of titanium,
aluminum, and magnesium are the most widely used. Titanium, which is 40 per cent lighter than steel, with a tensile
strength approaching that of most alloy steels, is widely used
because of its high strength-to-weight ratio. Aluminum and
magnesium are favored where lightness is a more important
factor than strength.

Steel has more diversified uses in the space program than any
other metal because it has a far greater range of applications.
Most grades of steel are easily shaped and lend themselves well
to fabrication, a factor of prime importance to engineers. Steel
combines ductility, toughness, strength, and resistance to heat
and corrosion to a degree unmatched by any other metal. By
careful adjustment of these properties, steel can be made in
more varieties to serve more purposes than any industrial
material known to man.

New steels and their applications in new ways indicate that
steel will be of growing importance in the space program. It
may even play a key role in all the things space engineers hope
to accomplish.

A steel called maraging steel has been produced for some
time. It is a special steel that is fairly soft when first made but

becomes very hard and strong as it ages. A new maraging steel with a high nickel content and lesser amounts of other alloys has made possible for the first time the construction of rocket cases as large as 260 inches in diameter.

The XB-70A Plane

Another achievement in aerospace technology is construction of the 2,000-mile-an-hour experimental supersonic aircraft, XB-70A. Its chief metal is an especially hardened stainless steel. The XB-70A, built for the U.S. Air Force, is their heaviest, fastest plane. It can absorb 630° F in sustained flight through the atmosphere. Sustained flight at high temperature is the key to supersonic planes flying at high Mach speeds. The prefix Mach is used to describe supersonic speed. When a plane travels at the speed of sound it is Mach1. Twice the speed of sound is Mach 2, and so on.

The XB-70A, in demonstrating that it can withstand 630° F, flying 2,000 miles an hour at an altitude of 70,000 feet, represents a major breakthrough in sustained high Mach flight. Research data gathered by the XB-70A will guide aircraft manufacturers in the construction of commercial supersonic air fleets.

To design the XB-70A, it was necessary to form a new concept of aircraft structure. Aluminum and magnesium, which sag at prolonged high temperatures, had to be discarded. The XB-70A is basically a stainless steel airplane. More than 70 per cent of its weight is stainless steel, 17 per cent is an ultra-strong alloy steel called H-11, and 9.5 per cent is titanium. Steel thus comprises over 87 per cent of the plane.

It became possible to construct a supersonic plane largely of steel for two principal reasons. (1) The stainless steel used in the framework and outer surfaces possesses both great strength and high heat resistance, whereas the H-11 steel is ultrastrong for engine mounts, landing gear, and other applications. The H-11 steel, refined by the vacuum-melting process, possesses great tensile strength and ductility. Both properties are essential in the engine mounts to "take" the shuddering vibration of a plane hurtling through space at high Mach speed. The same properties are required in the massive landing gear to withstand the impact of such a large plane as it touches the runway. (2) The rolling of stainless steel into foil as thin as 0.00075 inch made it possible to fabricate the steel into honeycomb sandwich panels. These strong, lightweight panels are the basic building blocks of the XB-70A.

Technological advances achieved in the construction of the XB-70A are already reaping a rich harvest in space vehicles, commercial aviation, and industrial applications. Stainless steel honeycomb panels serve as the heat shield of the Saturn I-B rocket which will boost the Apollo into its manned mission to the moon. The command module of the Apollo, which encloses the crew compartment, is composed of similar stainless steel panels for protection against the stress of liftoff and the searing heat of re-entry into the atmosphere. The same steels and the processing techniques used in construction of the XB-70A are being adopted by some of the major manufacturers of commercial aircraft in the United States. Stainless steel foil is also finding use in electronics, instrumentation, surgical supplies, recording tape, TV tubes, and in atomic energy equipment.

Steels of Even Greater Strength

There is the bright prospect that steels stronger than any known may be forthcoming in the years ahead. While man is lifting his eyes to the heavens in contemplation of outer space, he is discovering a new universe within the atom. Physicists say that the theoretical strength of metals is 1,000 to 10,000 times greater than their actual measured strength. It has been possible in the laboratory to produce pure crystals of molecular iron in the form of a filament with a tensile strength of 2,000,000 pounds per square inch. The strongest steels today have a tensile strength of 300,000 pounds per square inch, and new steels of 350,000 to 600,000 pounds per square inch are beginning to appear.

From a laboratory experiment to practical application is often a long, slow process, but the direction has been pointed out. The problem appears to be to get rid of the defects ordinarily existing in iron crystals, and by rendering them more nearly perfect, to produce steels of much greater strength. Studies are being pursued to produce steels twice as strong as any now known. If that goal is reached, steel will assuredly play a key role in the space program and greatly extend the metal's usefulness on earth.

Here on earth, steel will continue to serve as man's basic industrial metal as far as we can see into the future. This will be because of steel's great versatility and because there are almost limitless deposits of iron ore throughout the world— enough to support a machine civilization that will one day spread around the earth.

Looking into the more distant future, one of the steel industry's most important problems will be its source of energy for power. Steel production will be profoundly affected by the availability of cheap power from atomic energy. As mineral fuels become exhausted, the generation of power by nuclear energy will increase. After 1980, according to some estimates, it should become a significant part of total world production of power. By the year 2000, nuclear energy may account for one-third of total energy consumption. By the middle of the next century, most of our power may come from nuclear energy, with coal reserved almost entirely for the production of liquid fuels and chemicals.

Nuclear energy will one day be available at any place on the globe, at a fairly reasonable price. While it will be important to regions already industrialized, such as Europe, the United States, Canada, and Japan, it will be of greater importance to developing nations with poor energy resources. There, it will speed up the adoption of a machine economy and, in so doing, vastly increase the production and use of steel throughout the world.

The harnessing of nuclear energy to machines will not only bring about increased production of steel for its many uses in an industrialized economy, but will also create additional demands for the metal. More steel will be required for mining uranium and thorium ores. Additional steel will be needed for the construction of fuel-processing plants, where the mined ores are prepared for use in atomic reactors. An increased demand will develop for steels used in the recovery and safe disposal of radioactive materials.

The Long-Range Future

Nuclear energy as a source of power will affect the steel industry internally. By the time atomic energy drives the steel mills, they will be fully automated. We have been given a picture of the steel industry in the next century by the late Benjamin F. Fairless, former board chairman of U.S. Steel. He said that steel will be made in one continuous operation, using atomic energy as power. "Iron ore will move in at one end of the plant and finished steel products will emerge at the other, without intermediate processes. . . . Extruding will largely have replaced rolling to produce finished products." The order to make a specific kind and quantity of steel, the selection of raw materials, and the production of the steel will be handled by computers. The job of the few operators in the mill will be to see that everything flows smoothly. The operators will be assisted by maintenance crews trained to keep the system in perfect working order. At the rate automation is advancing in the steel industry, it may come ahead of nuclear power.

The day may eventually arrive when automation and nuclear power will constitute the foundation of a universal society —utilizing steel as its basic metal—a society in which "hunger, disease, fruitless toil, and early death" will have vanished from the earth.

Part III

A MODERN STEEL MILL

16

From Ore to Iron

A modern integrated steel mill is a great industrial complex occupying from several hundred to over 2,000 acres, and containing storage yards, power plants, iron- and steelmaking departments, and other facilities, all arranged for the orderly flow of operations—from the entry of raw materials to the shipment of finished steel products to customers. About 200 miles of railroad tracks are needed in the largest plants to transport various materials back and forth between different departments.

In addition to manufacturing facilities, a modern steel plant has testing and research laboratories, and a medical department staffed with doctors and nurses to give physical examinations to applicants for jobs and to treat injuries. The steel industry is noted for its low accident rate and has established many nonaccident records due to the intensive safety training given to employees.

Location of a Steel Mill

A number of considerations enter into the choice of a site for a steel mill. First, it must be a place where iron ore, coal, and limestone can be conveniently and economically assembled. Generally one or more of these materials must be transported a long distance by train or boat, or both, at considerable cost.

Following the discovery of large iron ore deposits in the Lake Superior region, steel companies in midwestern and eastern states found it more practical and economical to assemble their raw materials on or near the southern shores of the Great Lakes. Why did the companies not migrate closer to the ore mines instead of having to ship the ore nearly a thousand miles down the lakes? Because the sites on or near the lower lake shores offered two compensating advantages. The mills were near markets in large industrial areas. Steel is heavy and the cost of transporting it is an important factor in its price. Second, the mills were accessible to coking coal in the great Appalachian seams extending from Pennsylvania to Alabama. Over 90 per cent of all the bituminous coal used by the American steel industry is mined in Pennsylvania, West Virginia, Kentucky, and Alabama.

These considerations account for the concentration of America's steel centers in Illinois, Indiana, Ohio, New York, Michigan, and Pennsylvania, which today produce 75 per cent of all the steel made in the United States. Accessibility to the three raw materials for steelmaking also explains the location of a steel center in Birmingham, the largest in the South, and of steel centers in Texas, Colorado, Utah, California, and several other states.

Steel mills in the six states mentioned above, which rely on Lake Superior ores, now receive most of it in the form of *beneficiated* low-grade ores, which are preferred to the remaining richer ores. Most of the ore for eastern mills is shipped by boat from Canada, South America, and Africa.

The second important requirement for the site of a steel mill is good connections with main line railroads to bring in iron ore, coal, and limestone, and to transport finished steel products to markets. Relatively few American steel mills receive their ore directly at ports on the Great Lakes or the eastern seaboard. To the vast majority of the mills in the United States the ore is carried by rail. In addition to raw materials, large quantities of other supplies must flow constantly into the mill—fuel oil, scrap, alloying elements, and many others. The bulk of these arrive by rail. And, of course, finished steel products must be constantly shipped out.

Another requirement for the site of a steel mill is accessibility to fresh water. Enormous quantities of water are consumed in the various cooling operations of a large steel mill. It is estimated that 20,000 gallons are needed for every ton of finished steel produced. Much of the water is recirculated within the plant. Some plants clean the water before returning it to the river or lake from which it was withdrawn, so that the returned water is cleaner than when it was taken out.

The steel mill described in this and the next two chapters is not an actual mill. Few large steel mills contain all of the facilities mentioned. We will locate the mill on the southern shore of Lake Michigan in the Chicago area.

Raw Materials

We begin at the raw materials storage yards near the unloading dock. In the yards are immense mounds of iron ore and limestone. Just beyond them rise the towers of two blast furnaces. The coal arrives in long trainloads near the coke ovens, which are a short distance away.

At the dock, a 600-foot ore vessel has just come down the lakes from Duluth and is being unloaded. The pilothouse is at the bow and the propelling machinery is at the stern. In between, the deep holds of the ship are divided into compartments to prevent the ore from sliding about in transit. The average trip down the Great Lakes from Duluth is 850 miles.

The strange-looking machinery unloading the vessel is a Hulett electric unloader. It acts like a giant steel grasshopper, 90 feet tall, which dips its head into the hold of the ship, comes up with a mouthful of ore, moves back, and empties it into a receiving hopper. Five of these unloaders work on a vessel, bobbing up and down. If the ore is to be used right away, it is emptied from the hopper into railroad cars which carry it to the blast furnace stockhouse. If the ore is to be held in reserve, it is dumped near the dock. There the electric ore-bridge, running on tracks, gobbles up the ore in clam-shaped buckets and dumps it into one of the storage yards.

Limestone for the plant is quarried in upper Michigan and is brought down in cargo vessels.

Coke Ovens

The coke ovens are located in the area of the storage yards, the coal chemical-recovery plant, and blast furnaces. A coke oven is a steel structure about 20 inches wide, up to 14 feet tall, and 30 to 40 feet deep. The ovens are joined side by side in a series called a battery, which may consist of as many as one hundred ovens. On each side of an oven is a heating compartment of flues where gas is burned to supply the heat. The coal is charged into the oven through a hole in the top. It is dumped through the bottoms of cars moving back and forth on tracks above the ovens. Each charge contains about 20 tons of coal.

During the coking process the ovens are closed tight to prevent the admission of air. The heating chambers reach a temperature between 1,600° and 2,100° F. When bituminous coal is heated to such a temperature, away from air, it melts into a thick, bubbling, gummy mass, emitting great volumes of smoke and gas. Actually, the coal is distilled. What is left behind is a hard, gray, porous substance—coke,—which is about 90 per cent carbon.

It takes about seventeen hours to convert coal into coke. Then the doors at both ends of the ovens are removed, and a pusher machine arrives on tracks extending along one side of the ovens. It stops before each oven in turn, and a huge plunger pushes the coke out on the opposite side where it falls in a fiery cascade into a "hot car." The car is drawn by a locomotive a short distance to a quenching station where a spray of water plays on the coke. The coke is quenched because otherwise it might blaze up on contact with the air and much of it burn away.

Coal Chemical-Recovery Plant

In the days of beehive ovens the gases and vapors driven from coal in the coking process were allowed to escape into the air. Now they are brought from the ovens in large collector mains to the coal chemical-recovery plant for treatment. These volatile substances are made to yield gas, tar, ammonia, and light oil. The ammonia is treated with sulfuric acid to form ammonium sulfate, an excellent fertilizer. Further refinement of the light oil produces benzene, toluene, xylene, and solvent naphtha. The tar is distilled to produce naphthalene, creosote, pitch, and other compounds. Some of the gas is returned to the ovens to serve as fuel, some is piped to other departments in the mill, and some may be sold to outside customers.

These basic coal chemicals are later broken down into other compounds which are used in the manufacture of thousands of products. Benzene enters into the making of aviation gasoline, nylon, industrial solvents, printing ink, pharmaceuticals, perfumes, DDT, and dyes. A derivative of benzene is styrene, used as an ingredient in making synthetic rubber. Shiny lacquers, dyes, saccharin, and explosives such as TNT are derived from toluene. Naphtha is an important agent in dry-cleaning establishments. Naphthalene is familiar to everyone in the form of moth balls. It is also used in plastics, dyes, and insecticides.

Tar is used as a fuel in steelmaking furnaces and as a material in roadbuilding. Tar is also refined into a number of derivatives used in the manufacture of aspirin, flavoring extracts, wood preservatives, roofing and insulating materials, disinfectants, detergents, and many other products.

Pyridine, another coal chemical, is vital to the manufacture of sulfa drugs, certain vitamins, and water repellents.

The Blast Furnace

Three hundred years ago the largest blast furnaces were topped with a 30-foot stack and attained a weekly production of 25 to 30 tons of pig iron. The two giants we shall now examine have an overall height of 250 feet, and each can pour out over 2,000 tons of iron in twenty-four hours.

The large pipes that come down like arms from the top of the blast furnace carry off the enormous volume of gases liberated during the smelting process. The gases are led to a cleaning plant. A large portion of the gases is carbon monoxide, an excellent fuel. Some of it is burned in the stoves that

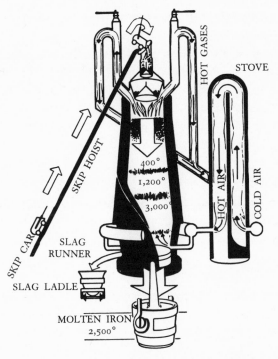

HOT GASES

STOVE

SKIP HOIST

400°
1,200°
3,000°

HOT AIR

COLD AIR

SKIP CAR

SLAG
RUNNER

SLAG LADLE

MOLTEN IRON
2,500°

How a blast furnace works. A skip car climbs the skip hoist and dumps its charge of raw material into the top of the furnace. The large pipes at the top carry off hot gases. At the right a heating stove supplies hot air for the furnace blast. The temperature rises as the charge descends into the hottest part of the furnace, where the iron melts and trickles to the bottom. *United States Steel Corporation.*

heat air for the blast, and some is piped to other departments in the mill. The heating stoves are the tall, round-topped towers between the two furnaces. The incline going to the top of the furnace is called the skip hoist. On it, busy little skip cars carry up raw materials and dump them into the top of the furnace. A blast furnace works day and night as long as it is in blast.

So much for an outside view of the furnace and stoves. The furnace itself, called the stack, is a steel shell about 100 feet tall, lined with heat-resistant brick. Even so, the brick lining is water-cooled to withstand the terrific heat within the furnace, which may reach 3,000° F or more in the hottest parts. From 10 to 12 million gallons of water a day are needed for cooling purposes. This is enough water for a city of 40,000 families, each consuming 250 gallons daily.

The Heating Stoves

A heating stove is divided into two compartments. One is a combustion chamber and the other contains bricks in a checker-board arrangement. Cleaned gas from the blast furnace is burned in the combustion chamber and the hot gas rises to the top and runs down through the bricks, heating them to a high temperature. When the bricks are sufficiently heated, the fire is turned off and air is blown through the stove in the opposite direction. Passing over the bricks, the cold air absorbs heat reaching 2,000° F or higher. Powerful blowing engines force the hot air from the stove into a large pipe called a bustle pipe, which encircles the furnace near the bottom. From the bustle pipe the hot air enters the furnace through a number of tuyeres spaced around the furnace.

Only one stove operates at a time. After the brickwork in an active stove cools off so that the air is no longer hot enough for the blast, the air is turned off. Then the air is blown through another stove that has been heated. After the second stove cools down, a third supplies the hot blast to the furnace. Thus the stoves take turns, ensuring a steady stream of hot blast for the furnace.

Charging the Furnace

Underneath the bottom of a skip hoist is the stockhouse, where iron ore, coke, and limestone are stored in separate bins.

They are dumped from above into the bins from bottom-dump railway cars or from conveyor belts. By reading dials in the control room, the operator in the stockhouse knows the level of materials in the furnace and regulates the charges accordingly. Only one material at a time is charged into the furnace.

Let us say that iron ore is to be charged in next. It flows from the bin into a scale car, so named because its load of raw material is weighed on a special set of scales. This is done almost with the care taken by a chemist in a laboratory. The scale car empties its load into a skip car at the bottom of the hoist. As one car goes up another comes down empty.

To produce 1 ton of pig iron requires about 1.6 tons of iron ore, 0.65 ton of coke, 0.28 ton of limestone, and from 1.8 to 2.0 tons of air in the blast. In other words, it takes nearly as much air by weight as raw materials to produce a ton of iron. For every ton of iron produced, the furnace gives off 3.5 tons of gases.

Within the Furnace

The hot blast rushing into the furnace at 350 miles an hour causes the coke to burn fiercely. Carbon in the coke unites with oxygen in the air to form carbon monoxide gas. Streaming upward through the charge, part of the gas takes oxygen from the iron ore to form carbon dioxide gas, reducing the ore to a spongy mass of iron. This, it will be recalled, was as far as the early smiths got with their Catalan forges and bloomeries, and they took out the lump and hammered it on their anvils to drive out the slag and cinders and compact the metal into wrought iron.

Now as the charge descends into the hottest zone of the furnace, where the temperature is around 3,500° F, the iron rapidly absorbs more carbon and melts. Drops of iron trickle into a pool, called the hearth, 3 to 4 feet deep at the bottom of the furnace.

Meanwhile the limestone becomes liquid too, and does its purifying, or purging, job. It takes up waste matter from both the ore and the coke to form molten slag. It also drips down, and because it is lighter than iron, it floats on top of the pool of liquid metal.

Every so often the slag is run off, flowing into a slag car or into a pit adjacent to the furnace. Crushed slag is sometimes used in road beds and is an excellent material for making some grades of cement. Slag is also used in mineral wool insulation.

Casting the Furnace

Every four or five hours the iron is run from the blast furnace, or cast, a term which arose in the earliest days of the blast furnace. The molten iron was then cast at the furnace site into various products such as pots, skillets, firebacks, and many others. Running the molten iron from the tap hole of the furnace was called casting the furnace, a term still applied to the blast furnace. But the word tapping is applied to steel-making furnaces. Originally a shed, or cast house, was built in front of the furnace for protection against all kinds of weather. The cast house serves the same purpose today. It is a building with an angular roof situated near the furnace.

To cast a blast furnace, a clay plug in the tap hole is drilled out, and a torrent of molten iron gushes forth. It flows down a curving trough in the cast house floor like a glowing white serpent, hissing and spitting a shower of sparks. At the end of the trough it flows into a bottle car, shaped somewhat like an elongated football. The car is so called because it is insulated like a giant thermos bottle to keep the iron in a molten state for delivery to steelmaking furnaces. From 150 to 350 tons of iron are cast at a time, depending on the size of the furnace.

Improved Blast Furnaces

Perhaps no unit of the steel industry has received as much attention in recent years as the blast furnace. Faced with rising costs, steelmakers have sought ways to increase furnace productivity. Not many years ago the output of 1,000 tons of iron a day was a great achievement, but now it is commonplace. New giants can produce over 2,000 tons in twenty-four hours, and it is expected that the production of 4,000 to 5,000 tons a day is not far off.

The annual production of pig iron has increased greatly in the last twenty years, and with fewer furnaces being used. The rise in output has been due partly to larger furnaces but even more to new practices which have raised the yield per furnace.

The most important new practice has been the increasing use of beneficiated iron ores. These are richer in iron, which means that more iron is obtained per ton of ore. Also the physical property of the ores is improved through agglomeration into pellets and nodules, which have the necessary strength and are of the right size to obtain maximum production rates.

Another improvement is the use of a hotter blast. Formerly the temperature of the blast was usually under 1,200° F. Now it goes as high as 2,100° F. The hotter blast has the effect of increasing the capacity of the furnace. Since less coke is required, the space saved by reducing the amount of coke allows more room for iron ore. By these and other practices it has been possible to double the production rates of the blast furnace.

Still greater production rates can be expected with the wider use of automation. It is already moving in. In one stockhouse the raw materials are withdrawn, weighed, and charged into

the furnace under the control of computers. At some future
date the blast furnace itself will be completely automated, and
heating stoves will be automatically self-adjusting to maintain
a uniform temperature in the furnace. Automated beneficiation
plants will produce agglomerated ores of uniform chemical
content and will contain their own fluxing agent, eliminating
the need for limestone. These and other controls will ensure
the production of pig iron of unfailing quality. Such changes
will come slowly in a step-by-step process but they will come.

Pig-Iron Production

Pig-iron production in the United States was 88 million tons
in 1965, the highest on record to that date. Canada also broke
all previous records in 1965 with 6,600,000 tons of pig iron.

About 95 per cent of the pig iron produced in the United
States and Canada is converted into steel. The remainder is
refined into various kinds of iron castings.

17

Making Steel

Four steelmaking processes are in use in the United States today—open hearth, basic oxygen, electric arc, and Bessemer. Their share of steel production, in the order named, is 72, 17.5, 10 and 0.5 per cent. The Bessemer process has practically disappeared in the United States, but is of historical interest as the first process for mass production of steel, ushering in the Steel Age.

The Bessemer Process

The Bessemer converter is a pear-shaped vessel with an open mouth at the top to admit the charge of molten iron and the escape of gases. The bottom contains from 150 to 200 holes for the admission of a powerful air blast. The capacity of converters ranges from 5 to 25 tons of steel per heat.

171

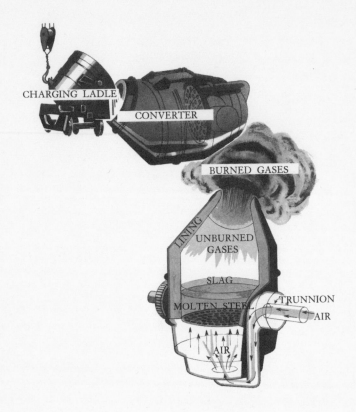

A Bessemer converter lying on its side to receive molten iron from a charging ladle. This position prevents the molten iron from clogging the air holes at the bottom. When the converter is tilted upright and the air is turned on, as shown in the cross section, oxygen in the air burns out impurities in the iron. Afterward a manganese compound is added to convert the iron into steel. *American Iron and Steel Institute.*

At the start of the operation, the converter rests on its side to receive the charge of molten iron poured into its mouth from a ladle. The vessel is on its side so that the liquid iron will not run to the bottom and clog the air holes. The converter is tilted upright and the air is turned on. It rushes in through nozzles in the bottom at the rate of 20,000 cubic feet a minute.

Flames and sparks belch from the roaring mouth of the

converter in a spectacular pyrotechnic display. Some minutes after the first volcanic outburst, reddish-brown fumes and long tongues of flame appear, indicating that the oxygen in the air is burning out the silicon, manganese, and other impurities in the iron. Next, the flames turn to yellow as the remaining silicon burns out, followed by long plumes of glittering white flame as the carbon is oxidized.

After twelve to fifteen minutes the flames die down. The converter is tilted on its side, the air is turned off, and the steel is poured into a ladle. Ferromanganese, an iron-manganese alloy, is added to remove excess oxygen and to restore the small amounts of carbon and manganese needed to convert the iron into steel.

The Open Hearth Process

The open hearth process has been the principal method of steel production in the United States during most of this century, at times accounting for 90 per cent of total output, but in recent years it has been losing ground while the basic oxygen process has been gaining. But open hearth furnaces still produce about 7 out of 10 tons of steel made in the United States.

An open hearth department consists of a row of perhaps ten furnaces, joined side by side. At the base of each furnace are brick-lined steel doors that can be raised by cables to permit the charging of materials. Viewed from the charging side, an open hearth furnace is not very impressive, but if you could put on a pair of open hearth goggles and look through a peephole in one of the doors, you would see metal bubbling at a temperature of 3,000° F.

The peephole serves two purposes. The foreman in charge of the furnaces, who is called the melter, can tell at a glance how the steel is progressing. But he relies on more than his own judgment. Samples of steel are frequently taken from the furnace for testing in the laboratory. They are removed through the hole in a long-handled ladle. The sample is poured into a mold on the floor where it is allowed to cool and solidify. The solidified sample is rushed to the laboratory. There it is analyzed in a spectrograph. Broken into a spectrum by an electric arc, each element in the steel sample emits a light of a different wavelength and character from the others. Within two minutes the technician can determine the percentage of each element in the sample, and in seven minutes he can send a complete report to the open hearth melter. Guided by the report, the melter adds whatever materials may be necessary to make the steel according to the composition ordered. So carefully is steel made that if a housewife prepared her ingredients for a cake with the care of a steelmaker, she would measure them not in spoonfuls and pinches but in thousandths of an ounce.

The open hearth furnace gets its name from its shallow, dish-shaped hearth wherein the materials are open to the sweep of the flames that melt and refine the steel.

How the Furnace Is Heated

The distinguishing feature of the open hearth furnace is its heating method. Above the hearth, at each end of the furnace, is a burner. Burning fuel and heated air unite at the burner and burst forth in long tongues of flame which play over the hearth. Hot air raises the temperature of the flames higher than cold air can. Various fuels are used such as natural gas, coke-oven gas, fuel oil, and tar.

At either side of the hearth, on a lower level, is a heating chamber lined with bricks in a checkerboard pattern. Only one burner is on at a time. Let us suppose that the flames are coming from the burner on the right side. The hot gases, after passing over the hearth, are drawn down through the checkers on the left side, heating those bricks. When the bricks are sufficiently heated, the direction of the flames is reversed. Cold air is led through the heated checkers on the left side, absorbing some of their heat. The heated air joins the flames at the left burner, and now the burned gases pass over the hearth and down the checkers on the right side, heating them. This reversal of flames and air takes place periodically.

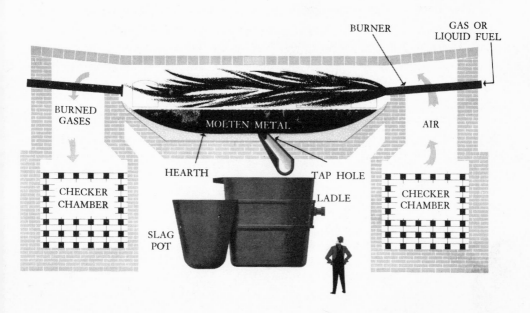

An open hearth furnace. Air, heated by passing through the hot, checker chambers, joins the flames and makes them burn at higher temperature. The burned gases escape through the other checker chambers, heating their bricks. The flow of air and gases is reversed periodically. *Bethlehem Steel Corporation.*

Charging the Furnace

To start making a heat of open hearth steel, limestone is charged in first. This is done mechanically. Along a set of tracks extending in front of the furnaces comes a complicated-looking apparatus called a charging machine. At the center sits the operator. He moves a lever and the machine reaches out a long steel arm which picks up a box loaded with limestone from a train of small cars stationed in front of the furnaces. The long arm pushes the box inside a furnace, turns it upside down to empty it, withdraws it, and returns it to its original position. Next iron ore is charged in the same manner, followed by steel scrap. The iron ore is added for oxidizing purposes.

Scrap

Scrap is an important material in the manufacture of steel. Almost as much scrap as pig iron is used in steelmaking furnaces. Scrap helps to conserve natural resources because it takes the place of iron ore. About half of the scrap comes from the steel mills themselves—the ends and sides of steel products as they are trimmed in various stages of manufacture. The rest comes from junked automobiles, worn-out rails, and various kinds of machinery, discarded steel products from the home, and odds and ends of steel that accumulate in industrial plants.

About an hour after the scrap has melted in the furnace, molten pig iron is added. It is charged into the furnace from a huge ladle suspended from an overhead electric crane. In a crackling shower of sparks the molten iron flows into a trough inserted in the open furnace door. Generally the furnace is charged with half scrap and half pig iron.

It takes about ten hours to make a heat of open hearth steel.

The time may be shortened somewhat by the injection of oxygen. This is usually done by inserting a tube called a lance through the roof of the furnace. The largest open hearth furnaces can produce 600 tons of steel in one heat, but the average is from 200 to 300 tons.

Tapping the Furnace and Teeming the Ingot

The steel is tapped on the opposite side of the furnaces. Let us imagine that we are in a deep pit below the level of the furnaces and are wearing open hearth goggles to protect our eyes against the glare of the incandescent molten steel as it gushes from the furnace. A huge ladle, capable of holding several hundred tons of molten steel, is swung from cables into position below the tap hole. A hand signal is given, and the tap hole is opened by an explosive charge. Steel of glittering whiteness pours into the ladle. Contact of the molten steel with the cold ladle causes sparks to rise and fall like a brilliant fountain over a wide area. After the steel has run out of the furnace, the slag comes last, spilling over the top of the ladle. Alloying elements are added either into the furnace or into the ladle.

The ladle is moved across the pit and stopped above the first of a row of ingot molds. These are tall iron jackets, resting on flat-bottom cars. A stopper in a hole at the bottom of the ladle is opened and the steel pours into the mold, filling it nearly to the top. The ladle moves on, filling each mold. This process is called teeming.

After the steel in the molds has solidified, the train of cars is moved to a yard outside. Here a massive pair of jaws called an ingot stripper catches hold of each ingot mold and lifts, or strips, it from the ingot. The stripped ingots, standing in a row, are a glowing cherry red. The ingot is the first solid form in which most steel is made.

The Electric Furnace

The great advantage of using heat generated by electricity in making steel is that the temperature can be regulated with closer precision than in any other type of furnace. In the electric furnace the temperature can be set at any desired figure and maintained there, which is of great importance in controlling the making of steel. That is why the electric furnace has long been associated with the manufacture of high-quality alloy steels. But as we learned earlier, the electric furnace is also used for making special carbon steels.

The electric furnace somewhat resembles a huge teakettle. Three graphite electrodes, extending through the roof of the furnace, carry the current to the charge. The roof can be removed for adding the charge, which consists almost entirely of steel scrap. The furnace can be tilted forward on rockers to pour out the molten steel and slag through a tap hole.

After the furnace has been charged, the current is turned on in the electrodes and they are lowered until arcs of electricity leap from them to the scrap. A noise like gunfire is heard within the furnace as the arcs leap and break. The intense heat generated by the arcs melts the scrap and the molten bath heaves as if it were boiling. The silicon, phosphorus, sulfur, and carbon are oxidized to form a slag which floats on top of the molten metal. At the proper stage, carefully measured amounts of alloying elements are shoveled in, elements such as nickel, chromium, tungsten, and vanadium, depending on the kind of steel being made.

It takes from four to twelve hours to make a heat of electric furnace steel, again depending on the type of steel being made, and on the size of the furnace. Then the furnace is tilted forward, allowing the metal to pour into a ladle. The steel is teemed in the same manner as open hearth steel. Electric furnaces usually produce from 150 to 200 tons of steel in one heat.

The Basic Oxygen Converter

Since its introduction in Austria in 1952 the basic oxygen process has spread rapidly around the world. By 1965 it was being used in twenty-nine nations. There are three chief reasons for the ready acceptance of the new steelmaking process: its speed, its relatively low cost of installation and operation, and its ability to produce a wide range of high-quality steels.

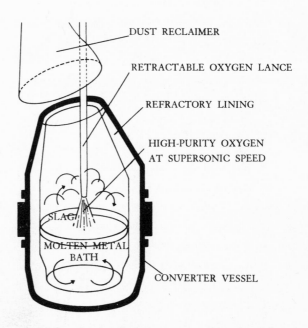

A basic oxygen converter. Molten iron and steel scrap are first charged into the converter. An oxygen lance is lowered to within a few feet of the charge and the oxygen is turned on. A violent outburst of smoke and gases issues from the mouth of the converter as the oxygen refines the iron into steel. *American Iron and Steel Institute.*

This combination of advantages is possessed by no other steel-making process. In addition, the new method can be used to produce steel on a small scale. The process is thus well suited to smaller nations with little capital, producing steel for the first time, which accounts for the eager adoption of the process by many such countries.

A basic oxygen converter closely resembles a Bessemer converter, but without the holes in the bottom for the admission of an air blast. Instead of air, pure oxygen is employed to refine the steel. It is fed into the mouth of the converter.

Like the Bessemer converter, the basic oxygen converter is tilted on its side to receive the charge, which consists of about 75 per cent molten iron and 25 per cent scrap. The vessel is then moved to an upright position and a water-cooled lance is lowered to within a few feet of the charge. The lance is connected to a tank containing oxygen kept under pressure.

The oxygen is turned on and flows through the lance to the charge. As the oxygen hits the molten iron the reaction is instantaneous and violent. Flames and dense clouds of smoke and gas erupt from the open mouth of the converter with a loud roaring noise. The gas and smoke are collected in a close-fitting shield and passed through cleaning equipment so that nothing escapes into the atmosphere.

The oxygen is dissolved in the molten bath and quickly oxidizes the silicon, manganese, phosphorus, and carbon. The carbon unites with the oxygen to form carbon monoxide gas which produces a vigorous boiling action of the entire charge. But all the carbon is not allowed to be oxidized. A very small amount must be retained to convert the iron into steel. The point at which the carbon reaches extremely low levels is easily recognized: The boiling action stops and the flames at the mouth of the converter die down. The oxygen is turned off, the lance is withdrawn, and the vessel is tilted on its side to permit skimming off the slag. The converter is tilted over farther so that the molten steel can be poured into a ladle. The entire operation takes about thirty-eight minutes. The average capacity of basic oxygen converters in the United States is 155 tons of steel per heat. The world's largest are two 350-ton capacity converters located in the United States.

18

Shaping Steel

Almost every steel product at some stage in its manufacture passes through a rolling mill. Steel at a temperature of about 2,200° F is a fairly soft material that can be shaped into various forms by passing it between two revolving metal cylinders. To roll steel into a flat form such as a sheet, the surface of the rolls must be slightly convex. By constructing grooves in the rolls, steel can be shaped round, square, octagonal, or in the form of the letter I or H, or other irregular shapes. The hot, soft steel is literally squeezed into the shape of the grooves through which it is passing.

An ingot of steel is formed into certain basic shapes and sizes for the convenience of customers. The builder of a bridge or athletic stadium will need girders and plates. The manufacturer of a car will need sheets for the body, pipes for the exhaust, rods for connections, and wire for the springs. And the customer can choose his steel from some three thousand grades, ranging from carbon steel through stainless steels and other alloy steels.

Semifinished Steel

To prepare steel for its thousands of uses, the ingot is first rolled into blooms, slabs, and billets. These are called semi-finished steel products because they constitute the stock from which finished steel products are made.

The Blooming Mill

After being stripped from their molds, the ingots have cooled off too much for rolling. They are reheated to rolling tempera-ture in a furnace called a soaking pit, where they are "soaked" in heat. When the blooming mill is ready to roll an ingot, one is lifted from the pit by a massive pair of tongs and transferred to a conveyor system consisting of small revolving steel rolls, known as a conveyor table. It is used throughout the mills to move steel from one rolling operation to another. The white-hot ingot now heads for the blooming mill.

Imagine that we are standing in a glass-enclosed booth called a pulpit, with a clear view of the roller table and the pair of rolls. Beside us are two men, the roller and his assistant, who operate the mill by pushing buttons and pulling levers.

A whistle is sounded, signaling the approach of the ingot. It comes along on the conveyor like a gigantic captive beast. Now it is within a few feet of the rolls. There is a loud thump as the ingot enters the rolls. The rolls grip the hot steel and pull it through, reducing its thickness slightly and making it longer. No sooner is the ingot through than it is brought back and passed through the rolls from the opposite side. This procedure is repeated, and after each pass the rolls are brought a little closer together. Every round trip or so, the ingot is turned on its side so that the sides are also thoroughly worked. After sixteen passes—in less than five minutes—the 25 by 27 inch ingot (in cross section) can be rolled down to a bloom 9 inches square.

Some blooming mills can also roll slabs and billets, but these are generally rolled on separate mills. Slabs are rolled from ingots in the same manner as blooms. The ingot is usually flattened into a slab 60 inches wide and 20 feet long.

The Billet Mill

Billets are rolled from blooms. Usually the billet mill is placed just after the blooming mill so that the ingot can be reduced to blooms and then to billets on its original heat.

The billet mill is a continuous mill, consisting of ten stands of two-high rolls arranged in a line. The grooves in each stand of rolls after the first stand are smaller and shaped more like a billet than the preceding pair. The hot bloom becomes longer as it is squeezed narrower by the grooves. To take up the increase in length, all the stands except the first are synchronized so that each pair of rolls turns faster than the pair before it. As a result, the steel moves continually faster as it progresses through the mill. The above description applies to all continuous rolling mills.

The first six stands roll the bloom into a long billet 4 inches square in cross section. If smaller billets are desired, the billets are transferred to the other four stands and rolled down to $1\frac{1}{2}$ inches square in cross section, and considerably lengthened. Both sizes of billets are sawed into lengths.

Finished Steel Products

Standard finished steel products are grouped in five major classifications: (1) flat products, (2) structural shapes and rails, (3) pipes and tubes, (4) bars and rods, and (5) wire. All but wire are rolled from one of the semifinished forms. Wire is drawn from rods. A number of specially finished products are also made, such as forgings and castings.

Fully half of all the steel products sold by the American steel industry is in a flat form. Forty per cent are sheet and strip and 10 per cent are plates.

Plates

There is only a slight difference between the thickest sheet and the thinnest plate. To distinguish between the two, it may be said that a steel plate is at least ¼ inch thick and over 8 inches wide. But a plate may be as thick as 25 inches and nearly 200 inches wide.

Plates serve structural and mechanical purposes beyond the strength of sheets. Plates are used in bridges, dams, heavy machinery, pressure vessels, railroad cars, atomic reactors, and the hulls and decks of ships.

Plates are rolled from slabs in several kinds of mills, one of which is a continuous mill. The function of these mills is the same—to reduce the slab to the desired thickness and width. A continuous plate mill contains six massive finishing stands, each with four rolls, one on top of the other, called a four-high stand. The top and bottom rolls are larger than the inner pair, and are used to back up the pressure exerted by the smaller rolls. From the last stand, the plate issues like a wide red carpet of steel, 80 feet or more in length.

Sheet and Strip

The building which houses a continuous hot-strip mill may be half a mile long. At the starting end is the slab storage yard, from which the slabs are taken one at a time and loaded onto a conveyor table. From this point on, the steel does not stop moving until it emerges as a long ribbon of strip at the other end.

The cold slabs first enter a long tunnel-shaped furnace through which they move slowly, a little distance apart. By the time a slab reaches the other end it is heated to rolling temperature. Leaving the exit door, the slab slides down an incline to a conveyor table which takes it to four preliminary, or roughing, stands. Here the slab is rolled considerably thinner and longer. It continues on to six powerful finishing stands, placed close together. Squeezed still thinner and longer and continually moving faster, the steel races from the last stand at speeds up to 3,500 feet a minute. The 6-foot, 25,000-pound slab has been stretched into a thin strip of steel a quarter of a mile long, and the entire rolling operation has taken only three minutes.

The strip of steel is usually wound into a coil, but it may also be cut into sheets. If the coil is to be cold-reduced, it is passed through a sulfuric acid solution to remove the scaly oxide that forms on the steel's surface during hot rolling. This process is called pickling. The coil of strip unwinds as it is fed through a continuous pickler, passing through tanks containing acid, followed by tanks of rinsing water. Emerging from the last tank the strip is rewound into a coil.

The main purpose of cold reduction is to reduce the steel in thickness. At the same time two other results are produced. The internal structure of the steel is altered so that after subsequent annealing the steel can be shaped cold in stamping presses. The surface of the steel is also given a satiny smooth finish which makes the steel suitable for applications where a lustrous finish is desired.

Much greater pressure is required to reduce steel in a cold condition than at hot-rolling temperature. To obtain the greater pressure four-high stands are employed, similar to those in a continuous plate mill. There may be as many as six of these powerful stands, driven by a total of more than 11,000 horsepower.

The front end of a coil of strip is threaded through the first stand of rolls and attains a greater speed than in the hot-strip mill. Moving at a rate of 4,500 to 7,000 feet a minute as it leaves the last rolls, the strip is rewound into a coil.

Cold rolling stiffens and hardens steel. To relax the steel and soften it internally so that it may be shaped cold in powerful stamping presses, the cold reduced coils are annealed. This operation is performed in an annealing furnace, where the steel is gently heated for some hours in the absence of air, which might oxidize the surface.

Electrolytic Tin-plating

Various coatings are applied to steel for protective or decorative purposes, or for both. The principal coatings are tin, zinc, porcelain enamel, aluminum, paint, lacquer, and vinyl. Tin is the most widely used.

Steel and tin make an ideal combination for the preservation of foods. Steel as thin as 0.006 inch provides adequate strength for cans, whereas a coating of tin about one-fortieth the thickness of a human hair gives protection against food contamination by acids. Tin plate is pleasing in appearance and may be decorated by lithographing or lacquering.

More than 6,000,000 tons of tin plate are manufactured in the United States annually. Most of it is produced by the electrolytic process. A large coil of cold-reduced sheet steel is fed into the machine and starts rapidly on its way. The instant the coil is nearly unwound, the front end of a new coil is welded to it, thus providing a continuously moving ribbon of steel.

The steel passes through various cleaning solutions to make its surface almost surgically clean so that the tin will adhere to it uniformly. The steel then goes through a tank containing a tin salt in solution. Here, an electric current causes the tin to be deposited as a metallic film on the steel's surface. The coated strip continues on through final processing which gives the tin plate a bright even surface.

Near the end of the line an automatic pinhole detector "observes" any tiny pinhole in the moving tin plate, while an automatic micrometer continuously measures the thickness of the tin plate. Both these instruments are synchronized with the flowing tin plate so that any defective sheet is automatically ejected at the end of the line where it is cut into sheets. Sometimes the tin plate is not cut into sheets but is wound into a coil and shipped in that form.

Galvanizing

Zinc is an excellent metal for protecting steel exposed to the weather and other corrosive conditions. Next to tin, zinc is the most widely used protective metal for steel. Coating steel with zinc is called galvanizing.

Familiar products made of galvanized sheet are ordinary water pails, garbage cans, and drums. Crimped into corrugated form, galvanized steel is easily recognized in rain gutters on houses, road culverts, and in roofing and siding. Galvanized steel finds wide use in grain storage bins and air conditioners.

Steel is galvanized by two different continuous methods. In one, a coil of strip is passed through a bath of molten zinc and recoiled. In the other, called electrogalvanizing, zinc is deposited on the steel electrolytically in much the same manner as in electrolytic tin-plating.

Structural Shapes and Rails

Almost everybody has watched a steel girder being hoisted into the air to form part of the framework of a building or bridge. Structural steel is essential to modern civilization with its business and industrial buildings, bridges, ocean liners, and other structures requiring the strength and durability of steel.

Steel for such purposes is made in what are called structural shapes. Viewed from one end, a structural shape may have the form of an H, I, L, T, U, Z, or numerous irregular shapes. Structural shapes are rolled from blooms and billets, depending on the size to be formed. The hot steel is passed through grooves in the rolls of appropriate design for the shape to be made.

Rails consumed a lion's share of steel produced in the United States during the great railroad building era of the last century. In the early 1900's rail production was still fairly large, representing one-fifth of all rolled steel, but the proportion has since fallen to 0.8 per cent. The decline in rail production in the present century is due to an ever greater share of transportation taken over by passenger automobiles, trucks, buses, and planes.

The introduction of high-speed trains traveling at 150 to more than 300 miles an hour, now under development, may herald a revival of passenger transportation between large cities, bringing a renewed demand for rails.

Rails are rolled from blooms. In a number of roughing stands the bloom is given the rough shape of a rail. In the grooves of the finishing stands the steel gradually assumes its final shape. It leaves the last rolls, a perfectly shaped rail, 130 feet long. It is sawed into lengths of 39 feet.

In order to prevent rails from developing minute internal cracks which might later enlarge dangerously in service, they are allowed to cool down slowly in the open air. Then they are placed in large insulated metal containers where they continue cooling slowly for a minimum of ten hours. Slow cooling has contributed greatly to the safety of rail travel. The rails are minutely inspected and put through a series of severe tests.

Pipes and Tubes

Without steel pipes and tubes, ranging from hypodermic needles to welded pipes over 12 feet in diameter, modern civilization could not go on. Steel pipe, as much as any single agency, has made possible the growth of large cities with underground pipelines to carry water, gas, and steam, together with sewer mains and conduits containing electric cables.

Petroleum is the lifeblood of a machine economy. The petroleum industry requires thousands of miles of steel pipes to raise crude oil from deep in the earth and transport it to refinery centers, which themselves are a maze of steel pipes.

Automobiles could not run and planes could not fly without steel tubes in fuel lines, exhaust systems, and other parts. The safety of a plane's touchdown depends on strong alloy steel tubes in the landing gear.

Steel tubes are used in milk pasteurizers. The refrigerants in refrigerators and ice-skating rinks are circulated in steel tubes. Steel tubes also serve a structural purpose in furniture, hospital beds, ship masts, and playgrounds.

The earliest pipes were made of bamboo, later of baked clay, and still later of pottery. Lead pipes were used extensively by the Greeks and Romans. In medieval Europe most pipes were made of hollowed logs. New York City's first regular waterworks, planned in 1774, was to have a network of 60,000 feet of hollowed logs, with an inside diameter of 9 inches, but the project was abandoned after the outbreak of the Revolutionary War.

Cast-iron pipes appeared as early as the fifteenth century and were later used extensively in water lines. The manufacture of wrought-iron pipe began in 1825 by what became known as the butt-weld process. A narrow strip of heated iron, called skelp, was passed through a funnel-shaped die. Entering the die, the edges of the skelp were curled into the shape of a pipe which emerged with a tight seam welded down its entire length. Later, steel replaced iron. Welded pipe is still made today but in a continuous process. A coil of skelp—actually narrow sheet steel—is fed into the mill and moves through a long furnace where it is heated to welding temperature. From the furnace the skelp passes through welding rolls which shape it into pipe with a welded seam.

Welded pipe has fairly thick walls. In the 1890's a demand arose for pipe with thinner walls that would weigh less but still be strong. In that era, when nearly everyone rode a bicycle, the demand for lighter pipes for the frames gave the chief impetus to making seamless pipe, generally referred to as seamless tube.

In the seamless process, a hole is pierced through the entire length of a round steel billet. You can demonstrate the principle involved by taking an eraser from a pencil and rolling it back and forth under a ruler or the handle of a knife. After a minute or two a cavity will appear in the center of the eraser.

This principle is applied in producing a seamless tube. A hot round billet is spun around rapidly between two revolving rolls, causing a cavity to form within the billet. The rotating rolls force the billet against a stationary blunt-nosed piercer, enlarging the cavity down the entire length of the billet. The result is a rough steel tube without a seam. Larger plugs are forced through the tube until its interior and wall thickness reach the desired dimensions.

Bars and Rods

Bars are one of the most widely used products of the steel industry. More bars are used in making automobiles than for any other purpose, but there is hardly an industry that does not use bars either to manufacture into other products or as part of a plant's machinery. The most common forms of bars are round, square, hexagonal, or octagonal, but bars are also made in many irregular shapes.

Large tonnages of bars are used to reinforce concrete for the construction of roads, buildings, bridges, and dams. Steel and concrete form a good partnership. Concrete can withstand great compression but it lacks strong resistance to pull, or tension. Steel has great tensile strength. By enmeshing a grid of steel bars in concrete, each does the work best suited to it. The next time you ride over a concrete highway, remember that you are also riding over steel.

Bars and rods are close cousins. A round bar and rod look alike. Bars and rods are rolled from billets on continuous mills. The billets pass through a series of grooves which shape the hot steel as in other rolling mills. Rods are used almost entirely for drawing wire.

Wire

Steel wire has 160,000 known uses. In diameter it ranges from 4/1,000 of an inch to nearly 1 inch. It can be made soft and pliable for paper clips, springy for springs, and so strong that a baby grand piano can be hung from a single strand of piano wire.

To meet its multitude of uses, steel wire is made to over ten thousand specifications, according to size, shape, grade of steel, finish, and coating.

In the home you will find wire in pins, needles, clothes hangers, strainers, refrigerator shelves, fan guards, and in door and window screens. Barbed wire and woven fences enclose farm lands and private property. Nails, tacks, bolts, nuts, screws, and rivets are made from wire. Some nails are so tiny that it takes 95,000 of them to weigh a pound. A giant spike made of wire weighs nearly 2 pounds.

Strands of steel wire are twisted together to make rope and cable for suspension bridges, and for hoisting purposes in construction, on board ship, and in manufacturing plants. A ski lift operates on steel wire cables.

In this mechanical age a steel spring is an indispensable go-between where energy cannot be transmitted conveniently in any other way. When a spring is compressed or stretched, energy is stored in it which is released when the spring is let go. Steel springs represent tireless muscles which speedily and faithfully do our bidding in thousands of ways, from door handles to mechanisms of almost every description. For their many functions, steel springs range from hairlike watch springs weighing 30,000 to the pound, to giant overhead garage-door springs.

The principle of wire drawing has not changed over the centuries. A rod is drawn through a hole, or die, of very hard material. The hole is tapered so that the exit end is of the exact size and shape of the wire to be drawn. To withstand the wear and pull of the rod, the interior of the die must be extremely hard. Tungsten carbide is generally used, but the diamond, the hardest substance known, is frequently employed in drawing very fine wire.

To start the operation, a reel containing a long coiled rod is placed near the wire-drawing machine. The end of the rod is tapered so that it can pass through the die like thread through a needle. The end is fastened to a rotating drum called a block. As the motor-driven block revolves, it draws the rod through the die and winds the wire around itself. After one passage through the die the rod becomes wire. Almost all wire is drawn through more than one die. The coil of wire is taken to a die of smaller diameter, drawn through it, and then drawn through still smaller dies, until the wire is of the exact size for its intended use. This is called single-draft drawing.

Wire is also drawn continuously. It passes without stopping through a series of dies, each one of smaller diameter, the number of dies depending on the size of the wire ordered.

Forgings and Castings

Vulcan, the mythological Roman god of metalworking who forged the thunderbolts for Jupiter, has come down through the ages as the patron of the smith. Forging was the first method used to shape hot metal and was performed by the mighty smith with his ringing hammer.

The first mechanical forging began with the water-driven trip hammer. It underwent little change for five centuries, except for larger hammers, until the early stages of the Industrial Revolution. Forgemen were asked to shape larger masses of iron for parts of machinery than could be produced by water power. The problem was solved temporarily by the use of steam power to raise a heavier hammer. The hammer obtained the force of its blow by simply falling on an anvil. This was called a drop forge.

It was not very long before the falling hammer proved inadequate to forge the still larger products which customers were ordering. This deficiency was corrected by the double-acting hammer, in which steam power drove the downward stroke of the hammer, greatly increasing the impact of its blow.

The ingot, first of iron and later of steel, was the basic stock for forging large products. As steel ingots grew larger, the steam hammer could no longer forge the more massive blocks of steel. The answer was provided by the hydraulic press which shapes hot metal by pressure instead of by hammering. The term hydraulic applies to a machine or device employing the force exerted by water or other fluids under strong pressure. In an hydraulic press, the metal is squeezed into shape within a die consisting of two parts. The lower half is in a stationary block, on which rests the hot ingot to be forged. The upper half of the die is contained in the underface of a ram, which is lowered onto the ingot. Under powerful hydraulic pressure, the ram squeezes the hot metal into the shape of the complete die.

The drop hammer and the double-acting hammer are still used today, the first for relatively small forgings and the second for somewhat larger forgings. But the largest ingots, weighing up to 600,000 pounds, are forged in hydraulic presses that can exert pressure as high as 50,000 tons.

Some of the largest forgings are electric generator shafts, steam turbine rotors, and propeller shafts for ships. Heavy forgings are also made for cyclotrons, or atom smashers, and for nuclear reactors.

Casting

Next to forging, casting is the oldest method for shaping hot metal and was begun far back in antiquity. Castings fill a very important need in a machine economy by making possible the formation of products which are too large or irregular in shape to be forged or produced on rolling mills.

Iron castings answer a variety of needs and are produced in several different grades, depending on their use. Some iron castings are of varying degrees of hardness and others are malleable. The familiar bathtub, washbasin, and sink may be hard iron castings given an enamel coating. Malleable iron castings possess both strength and ductility, and find application where a small degree of give is necessary. The widest use of malleable iron castings is in automobiles—steering gear housings, differential cases, brake pedals, and various brackets.

The principle of casting is the same whatever the metal cast. Let us say it is steel, to be cast into a frame for a steam turbine. The first step is to make a wooden or metal pattern of the exact shape of the frame. The pattern is placed in a mold, and sand is packed around it. The top of the mold is lifted and the pattern is removed. The top of the mold is put back in place, and molten steel is poured through an opening in the mold. The steel solidifies into a casting shaped like the frame.

The solidified casting is removed from the mold and cleaned of any sand or other particles adhering to it. The casting is then machined to give it a smooth surface and correct measurements.

Automation Again

In Part III automation was touched on only once and then in connection with improved blast furnaces. Elsewhere it was felt that the processes described in Part III could be more easily understood if the discussion were confined to their fundamental principle. Automation does not change basic principles. Computers make existing processes work faster, with greater precision, closer control over the quality of the product, and at lower cost. By reason of greater precision and control, the outstanding advantage of computers is improvement in the quality of products. It is primarily to improve the quality of its products that the steel industry is automating its operations with computers. It can be expected that existing and new processes will be computerized wherever possible.

In a word, machines directed by computers can produce a better product than they can under direct human control.

INDEX

Agglomeration, 138–139
Alloy steels, 77–95,
  in antiquity, 19
  definition of, 77
  future demands for, 86
  space vehicles in, 150–152
  vital to machine economy, 77
Alloying elements, 86–95
Ancony, 30
Annealing, 186–187
Atomic-Space Age, atomic-auto-
  mated steel mill in, 154–155
  problems of strength and heat,
    149–150
  steel for Space Age, 150
  steel of greater strength, 153
  technology outdistances metal-
    lurgy in, 148
Automation, 122–127, 196
Automobile, development of all-
  steel, 97–99

Bars, 30, 191–192
Basic oxygen process, history of,
  111–113
  operation of, 179–181
  share of steel production, 171
Bellows, 5, 14, 23
Bells, church, 24–26
Bessemer, Henry, 45–54, 111, 122
Bessemer process, America, established in, 53
  invention of, 45–52
  operation of, 171–173
  and railroads, 53–54
  share of steel production, 171
Billet, continuous casting of,
  119–120

Billet (*Continued*)
  from rolling mill, 183–184
Blast furnace, beginning of, 22–24
  coke replaces charcoal in, *see*
    Coke
  computerized, 123
  improved efficiency, 145, 169
  modern operation of, 164–170
Bloom, 30, 119, 183–184
Bloomery, 22
Bronze Age, 4, 7–9
Budd, Edward G., 97–99

Cannon (cannonballs), 26
Carbon, effect in iron, 13, 15, 28
  function in blast furnace, 167
  in pig iron, *see* Pig iron
Carbon steel, grades of, 76–77
Carburizing, 15
Carnegie, Andrew, 62–63, 65–75
Casting, blast furnace, 168
  continuous, 118–121
  first metals, 6–8
  iron, *see* Cast iron
  steel, 195
Cast iron, conversion to wrought
    iron, 28–30
  early, 24–28
  modern, 170
Catalan forge, 20–22
Cementation, 18–19, 41, 114
Charcoal, in early furnaces and
    forges, 13–15, 29
  how made, 35
  replaced by coke in blast fur-
    nace, *see* Coke
Coal chemicals, 163–164

Coke, consumption per ton of
    iron, 167
  ovens, 162–164
  replaces charcoal in blast fur-
    nace, 35–37
Continuous hot-strip mill, see Roll-
    ing mill
Copper Age, 4–9
Cort, Henry, 38–39
Crucible process, 18, 41–42, 45, 49,
    114
Cupola, 27–28

Darby, Abraham, 36

Electric process, history of, 107–
    108
  operation of, 178–179
  share of steel production, 171
Electrolytic tin-plating, see Tin
    plate

Faraday, Michael, 78
Finery, 29
Finished steel, classifications of,
    184
Firebacks, 27
Forging, iron, 13–15, 37–38, 40
  steel, 194–195
Frick, Henry Clay, 69–70
Furnaces, basic oxygen, see Basic
    oxygen process
  Bessemer, see Bessemer process
  blast, see Blast furnace
  bloomery, 22
  early iron-smelting, 14
  electric, see Electric process
  open hearth, see Open hearth
    process

Furnaces (Continued)
  puddling, 39–40, 114
  stückofen, 22–24

Galvanizing, 188
Gary, Judge Elbert H., 70, 73–74
Gold, 3–4, 82

Hittites, 12
Huntsman, Benjamin, 41–42

Ingot, 116–117, 119, 182–183, 194
Iron, bar, standard product, 30
  cast, see Cast iron
  products, early, 16, 25–28, 30–34,
    38
  first knowledge of, 10
  pig, see Pig iron
  smelting of, see Smelting
  wrought, see Wrought iron
Iron Age, 11–12, 16, 147
Iron ore, beneficiated low-grade,
    137–139, 145, 161, 169
  change in American exports
    and imports of, 136–137, 139,
    145–146
  consumption per ton of iron, 167
  jasper, 138–139
  Lake Superior, see Lake Su-
    perior region
  taconite, 138–139
  world reserves of, 133, 136, see
    also table, 140–144

Jasper, 138–139

Kelly, William, 45–48, 50, 52–53

Lake Superior region, 59–65, 137–
    139, 145, 160
Limestone, 59, 162, 167

Merritt brothers, 61–63
Mesabi iron ore range, 59, 61–63
Meteorites, 10–11
Morgan, J. Pierpont, 70–74
Mushet, Robert, 45, 51–52, 79

Nails, 33–34
"Natural" steel, 19

Oliver, Henry W., 61–62
Open hearth process, invention of,
    54–55
  operation of, 173–177
  share of steel production, 171
  surpasses Bessemer, 56–57
  threatened by basic oxygen proc-
    ess, 113
Ore vessel, 64, 162

Pig iron, carbon in, 50
  conversion to steel, 50
  conversion to wrought iron, 28–
    30
  materials required per ton pro-
    duced, 167
  origin of term, 28
  production, 170

Quenching, 15

Rails, railroad, 53–54, 57, 189
  mill for producing, see Rolling
    mill
Rockefeller, John D., 62–63
Rods, 191–192
Rolling mill, blooming, 183–184
  billet, 184
  continuous hot-strip, 100, 102–
    104, 123, 185–186

Rolling mill (Continued)
  cold reduction in, 104–105, 186–
    187
  cold rolling in, 104
  early history of, 37–38
  grooved rolls in, 38–40, 182, 184,
    192
  hand sheet, 99–102
  plate, 185
  structural, 189
  rail, 189

Schwab, Charles, 69, 73–74
Scrap, 176
Semifinished steel, 119, 183
Sheets, from continuous hot-strip
    mill, see Rolling mill
  first rolling of, 34
  from hand sheet mill, see Roll-
    ing mill
  uses of, 104–106
Slab, 119, 183, 185–186
Slitting mill, 33
Smelting, definition of, 4–5
  discovery of, 4–6
  early iron, 12–14
Spiegeleisen, 52, 91
Stainless steel, 82–84, 150–152
Steel, alloy, see Alloy steels
  carbon, see Carbon steel
  characteristics, range of, 150
  consumption of, per capita, 57,
    129, 132, see also table, 130–
    132
  foil, 110–111
  machine tool, 78–80
  strength of, 149, 152–153
Steelmaking, in antiquity, 17–19
  Bessemer, see Bessemer process

Steelmaking (*Continued*)
  cementation, 18–19, 41, 114
  crucible, *see* Crucible process
  electric process, *see* Electric process
  "natural," 19
  nations, new, 129
  open hearth process, *see* Open hearth process
  oxygen process, *see* Basic oxygen process
  review of processes, 113–114, *see also* table, 115
  wootz, 17–19, 41, 77–78
Steel mill, modern integrated, location of, requirements for, 160–161
  from ore to iron in, 161–170
  future atomic-powered, 154–155
  making steel in, 171–181
  shaping steel in, 182–196
  size of, 159
Steel production, American, nineteenth century, 53, 57
  American, by processes, 113–114, *see also* table, 115
  by countries, 133, *see also* table, 134–135
Structural steel, 188–189
Stückofen, 22–24
Steel Age, 45, 57, 75, 86, 148

Taconite, 138–139
Teeming, 177
Tempering, 15
Tilt hammer, 25, 30
Tin plate, early history, 34–35
  by electrolytic process, 109–110, 178–188
  ultrathin, 110
Tubes and pipes, history and uses of, 190
  manufacture of, 191
Tytus, John Butler, 102–104

Vacuum refining, 114, 116–118

Water, power, early iron industry, 23, 25
  consumption per ton of steel, 161
  consumption in blast furnace, 166
Wire, history of, 32–33
  drawing, modern, 192–194
  uses of, 192–193
Wootz steel, 17–19, 41, 77–78
Wrought iron, early production of, 13
  characteristics of, 14–15
  conversion from pig iron, 29–30

XB-70A supersonic plane, 151–152